MY SWEETHEART

YOU are no longer my Sweetheart

Pilar Cerón Durán

The Muse of the Atacama Desert, Chile

Cover and back cover design: *Gisela BC Design*

English interpreter: Ariadna Carobene. Workana

Editor: Maite Ayala https://www.facebook.com/maite.ayala.77

Dedication

This book, called **My Sweetheart** and subtitled **YOU are no longer my Sweetheart**, is dedicated to all those who, despite the years that have passed, still keep the love of their life alive in their hearts and thoughts; a loved one, probably an idealized product of the impetus of youth and the experiences of love and passion lived, considered one of a kind and almost perfect, where no other person on the face of the earth is capable of making them feel and live the magic of that irreplaceable, perfect and almost sacred love. The story of a new couple and the relationship between a family and children, where love, happiness and stability reign, becoming imperfect with the presence and shadow of that great and unique passion that could turn a fairy tale into reality.

I dedicate this book to those who read and immersed themselves in the story of Esmeralda and her Sweetheart; may I be able to provide sparks of hope and strength to ease the way into making the grand decision of risking everything in order to reunite with their great love, or have the courage to leave it in the past as a wonderful dream.

Acknowledgments

First and foremost, I thank life for it's, the failures, mistakes, unfortunate experiences losses, and the sea of tears, anguish, suffering and pain received. An accumulation of extraordinary experiences and learning that I recognize from the depths of my being, allowing me to see the world devoid of fears, angst, insecurities, and above all, lighter than that burden of prejudices and limiting traditions. All of this has transformed me into a free woman, an expert in resilience and in living free of attachments, an amour that has forged a thick skin on an almost invincible woman, risk taker, which has empowered her to be more audacious than ever, for whom there are no no's or limits, where challenges become her adrenaline in each awakening.

About the author

Pilar Cerón Durán

The Muse of the Atacama Desert, Chile

A writer of Chilean nationality, she was born in Pichidegua in 1963. She is a social worker by profession and has a master's degree in business administration. After once again experiencing firsthand death and social isolation as a result of the Coronavirus pandemic, she devoted herself to her passion in letters and in her meteoric path as a writer. In a period of less than a year, she has published three literary works, reaching the position of best seller on Amazon and in January 2022, making a successful literary tour in Chile; donating copies of her works to public libraries wherever she went: Chile, Australia, Germany and England, contributing to the promotion of reading and free access to books.

Links to contact the author

Email: pilarceronduran@gmail.com

Facebook Fan Page: https://acortar.link/ZAax1

Instagram: https://www.instagram.com/

YouTube channel: https://n9.cl/q8iw1

WhatsApp: https://wa.me/qr/CIUJYBAU73CWK1

MY SWEETHEART

YOU are no longer my Sweetheart

Pilar Cerón Durán

The Muse of the Atacama Desert, Chile

Introduction

My Sweetheart, a novel of love, intrigue, suffering, sleeplessness and challenges subtitled: *YOU are no longer my Sweetheart*, has a strong, precise and convincing message that only an empowered person can proclaim from the rooftops when facing the reality of a relationship filled with love, happiness and passion. A story of a person aware that life is to be enjoyed lavishly and with no time to waste beside their sweetheart, but without the taste of the exquisiteness and aroma with which it captivated them. All that's left is to open the door and set out on a path of no return, ending a chapter in a healthy way. Who more than the captivating Esmeralda, the protagonist of the unforgettable literary work "*The Pilgrim Bride. Is a second marriage better than the first?*" is capable of giving such a masterful sentence?

A woman of great strengths faced with one of the greatest dilemmas of her life upon discovering that her great love from the past, still present in her heart, is still in London. She is willing to risk everything to reunite with him, because she knows that she is destined to be with him. But there is a small big problem: her 21st century prince.

Esmeralda, an empowered woman and lover of her freedom, who feeds off of challenges, regardless of the fact that for most people they're dreams which are impossible to achieve, and for others, true madness.

She decides to leave everything behind, her beloved husband, her home and the stability of a family. Will Esmeralda be able to overcome the obstacles and ignite the passionate flame of love from twenty years ago?

Determined to consummate her long-awaited and elusive love, added to the fact of having a near death experience by contracting coronavirus, she embarks on a new adventure with her magical red shoes.

And you, would you be willing to risk everything... to reunite with your great love from the past or from youth? There isn't anything or anyone that can stop Esmeralda, nor will she die without once again savoring the sweetness of her Sweetheart.

I t was one of those days when something bothers you without being able to identify what it is; no matter how hard you try to decipher the enigma, it becomes a real waste of energy, until it clicks...

–Mmmm, I wonder how he's doing…it's been several years now since the last time we communicated by email… Where could my Sweetheart be? Is he perhaps still in London or has he returned to his homeland, to the bustling city of Chicago? Or maybe he moved to Switzerland, he used to comment that it was the best country in the world to live in, with one of the highest rates of quality of life in the world, a country where every decision that the government makes is first consulted with its citizens, where the per capita index is one of a kind to the point that any developed country would like to have. Well, no way to know where he is... I have no way of getting in touch with him... I don't even have his email. Ever since he changed jobs, I lost every way of contacting him... Ah, I know, Google. Yes, Mr. Google knows everything; let's see what it says...

Esmeralda writes in the Google search bar the name of the person she was inquiring about, and to her great joy, or rather, to her great regret, a dozen profiles appear with the name Todd Meyer, to be exact, 18, a big number.

Euphoric by the discovery and for the real possibility of finding him, and bearing in mind that NO's don't exist for her, she takes on the task of reading each of the profiles, finding people from all over the world, mostly from the United States, some with and others without photographs. In that, an artist catches her eye, a very famous singer who coincidentally had the same name, obviously it wasn't her Todd because he's an intellectual and not into music.

After a few hours of frantically searching and not having any positive results, she comes up with another great idea, to search on Facebook. Yes! If Mr. Google doesn't know, then surely Facebook will help find his whereabouts. She repeats the same exercise; she rewrites the name of her beloved Todd Meyer in the Facebook search bar and the situation repeats itself: countless people with the same name appear, but that doesn't make her give up. In the arduous task of looking for her Todd, it's easy to discard people from their photographs and professions. However, several of the profiles don't have pictures, or worse still, are private accounts, therefore, restricting access to more information than just the name or a simple profile.

Esmeralda, with the ferocious obsession to find him, and filled with adrenaline, doesn't give up and sends a message to all the Todd's who appeared without a photograph:

–Hi Todd, I'd love to hear how you're doing. How about getting coffee some time? –she concludes by revealing who she is: Sincerely, Esmeralda.

Feeling a little calmer, she relaxes while waiting for a response, even though he was a man known to be pragmatic, intellectual and reserved, completely removed from social media since he considered it was only for teens. Esmeralda goes down to the kitchen, prepares a cup of coffee and drinks it in the garden. She begins evoking erotic and sensual encounters filled with passion and lust, characterized by insatiable intensity and devotion due to the containment during absence, even more fiery when dealing with absences longer than usual, two or three months, and not to mention the eruption that occurred in those unforeseen trips, short and fleeting like lightning. The distance and the days didn't count when planning a new encounter. It didn't matter where he was, be it at a conference or an international meeting, there she flew at the speed of light. "A woman's panties pull more than a yoke of oxen", her dear friend Juan Manuel would say in popular jargon, although in this case, it would be "A man's boxers pull more than a yoke of oxen".

Time goes by as if she had magically forgotten her purpose, until one day by chance, when going on her Facebook page, a notification from Messenger catches her attention, a messaging app associated with Facebook which she had entered on certain occasions. She was curious about the number of unread messages and came across the following:

–Hello, my dearest Esmeralda. How are you? Did you move back to Chile or are you still living in the UK?

Wow wow wow! This made the hairs on her legs stand up, which trembled even though she was sitting in front of the computer. She couldn't believe what she was reading. Yes! She had finally managed to get in touch with her beloved Todd, her Sweetheart. The tachycardia and euphoria didn't prevent her from responding instinctively and viscerally:

–Hello, dear Todd. I'm still living in London. –I'm so happy to hear from you.

–How are you? Where are you living now? Did you move to Chicago or are you still in London?

There were so many questions that bombarded her mind and agitated her heart. From that day on, nothing mattered in her current life, displacing everything, absolutely everything, by a boomerang of memories, of a sublime, magical love, dreamt by many; A natural and genuine love, eyes glistening with light and

4

smiles overflowing with joy, just like children's faces when receiving the long-awaited toy on Christmas and on their birthdays. It was a love like no other, passionate and fulminating, almost perfect, even with the physical distance that separated them and the language barrier, although not speaking the same language wasn't essential because their love language was perfect and magical. Love and great sex were what prevailed and united them. They were days and weekends of making love over and over again, in an inexhaustible and insatiable way, to the point of laughing and joking seriously that the Kama-sutra should be reissued with their new positions. Amen to the fact that gyms and diets should be completely discarded, what better exercise than making love again and again to show off a model figure, toned limbs, lush skin, shiny bright hair envied even by the stars. Oh! And the sleepless nights, aches, anguish and lack of energy completely extinguished, and all thanks to the fulfilling love and nights of pleasure... nights? Not even close, they were days, afternoons, nights, early mornings and dawns. In short, love is love and making love when you are fully in love, turns out to be from another dimension. You lose count of how many times you gave yourself during the same day, savoring the humidity, the aroma and the moans of explosion from an earth-quaking orgasm fogging up the windows of the room, witness to the fervent pleasure and carnal surrender, orgasms that penetrate walls generating the vigilance and envy of the guests of adjoining rooms of furtive hotels, targeting executives and business passengers, who mostly travel alone.

That's how they began talking once again, weighted with such vehemence and passion.

In their second chat, anxious to know about each other's lives and what had happened to them during those endless twenty years in absence, they spent the night talking...

–Yes, I still live in London; however, I'm planning to move to Chicago or perhaps Italy. Yes, I dream of living in Italy. But tell me, what has become of your life, my lovely Esmeralda? –Todd asks.

–I've been living in London since October 2013 –Esmeralda replies.

–Really? You live in London?

–Yes, I live in London –she replies with overflowing joy as she realizes that they were both in London, shortening the distances and increasing the chances of a reencounter.

–This is wonderful, the two of us living in London –he says with vibrant joy at the realization, anxiously continuing his semi-interrogation, wanting to know everything about her–. Oh no, it's just that I can't believe it; tell me, tell me, what are you doing? Why are you living in London?

—I'm working at a preschool. Yeah, I work with children…

—Congratulations! I know how much you love children.

—Yes of course, I enjoy working with children very much; however, my greatest wish is to be a social worker. You know how much I love my profession and how much I like to help people.

—Yes, I know. But I don't understand why you're living in England and not in Chile, please tell me.

—Sure, okay. I'm living here because I got married. Yes, I married an Englishman.

He interrupts her:

—Oh yes, I remember, I saw on Facebook when you got married. A friend who knew about our relationship told me and showed me the photograph of you in your wedding dress; that news completely destroyed me. It was impossible not to feel guilty, regretful and furious about not marrying you when we were completely in love. Mmm, how stupid I was; I will never forgive myself. Even that day, yes, your wedding day, I wanted to fly to Chile, kidnap you and take you with me to Chicago or bring you here to London, to live together and make love every day. Mmm, I even sent you an email that you never replied to.

Being in contact through Messenger didn't prevent them from perceiving the deep pain and anguish of which they were prey. It hurt more than they could bare, reproaching each other for not having fought for their love when life gave them the chance to. They were united by the uncontrollable passion of a crushed love that intoxicates two souls in one body, uniting them by the scorching fire of passion, sweaty, panting and insatiable hunger. Upon meeting again in this earthly life, after the certainty of having shared a love forbidden by their parents in past lives, each encounter being a paradise dreamt by every couple in love, both young adults, with their lives resolved professionally, they could have easily made the decision to bind their lives to eternity. However, love and concern for his teenage children prevailed when it came to making his long-awaited dream come true. The pragmatism with which he used to make decisions led him to hug his beloved Esmeralda for the last time, at the international airport in Santiago de Chile, before heading back to London. It was a hug that gave him everything in return, stripping away from the love, passion, idealism and admiration with which she loved him, looking at her with infinite sweetness and at the same time, trying to stay calm and collected. His almond-coloured eyes reddened and turned into a stream of tears, which no matter how hard he tried to hold back, flowed like a stream down his cheeks, showing his great pain. He took a deep breath, emitting two words that echoed in Esmeralda's ears that refused to listen and even less, to accept what she was experiencing:

–It's over!!! –It's over!!!

Esmeralda, despite the fact that she had never heard those two words in English, didn't have the need in mastering the Anglo-Saxon language, her heart understood the meaning perfectly. She broke down in a sea of tears of blood that burst from the irreparable wounds that he had left in her heart, submerging her into utter misery and desolation.

They were days, weeks and months of non-stop crying. Her daughter Renata, and Kirana –a young American who was staying at Esmeralda's house as a student exchange, replacing her daughter Victoria, who was in Colorado, United States– tried to soothe her pain, caressing her hair and drying her tears, while she sat for hours, days and nights in front of the computer, waiting to receive an email from her beloved Todd. She would look at his pictures over and over again. The days became nights and the nights became dawns re-reading the passionate emails and reliving every detail in each of their encounters. The passion had been sublime and maddening. She remembers that in one of their encounters in São Paulo, he asked her to go to the airport to wait for him wearing only a raincoat. When that morning arrived, after taking a bath, she covered her body from head to toe with a moisturizing lotion, perfumed her body, put on makeup, brushed her hair, and took one last look at the huge mirror that covered both closet doors, flaunting her well-deserved vanity, sensually contemplating the beauty of her contoured and beautiful body. She looked radiant, with a velvety shine that highlighted the beauty of her breasts, delicate hips and fine legs. At 35 years old she looked 20. In that, the phone in her room rang, it was the hotel receptionist:

—Ms. Esmeralda, your taxi is here.

—Thank you, I'll be right there.

She quickly opens one of the closet doors, takes her long golden sand-colored raincoat, puts it on buttoning it up to her chest area, takes her bright green purse and closes the door. Like a diva, she walks to the hotel lobby where a man was waiting to accompany her to the taxi. The journey to the airport was endless, the desire to meet her great love again made her vibrate like a teenager in love, with the typical sensation of butterflies in her stomach, and on the other hand, enjoying the adrenaline that caused her to feel and act in a daring and audacious way, to the point that she could explode in a thunderous orgasm upon seeing and exchanging glances with her beloved Todd. Shining bright when running to meet him, she quickly unbuttoned her long golden sand-colored raincoat, the only garment that covered her beautiful and youthful body, embracing each other with overflowing passion and madness that alerted all her senses and

10

organs. Panting and controlling her hands to avoid showing her desire in the taxi, they barely managed to make it to the hotel. They opened the bedroom door and throwing off the raincoat while he finished taking off his pants, a task he had begun in the elevator, they merged into a single body, bursting into total and absolute surrender, a sublime rapport of two beings who love each other body and soul…

Wow, that's how their encounters were, just three days of inexhaustible and insatiable love, where every second was precious time that they took full advantage of… Breakfast consisted of two things, one was waking up loving each other with more passion than the night before and the other, was the early morning saying goodbye and welcoming a new dawn. Then, a shower for two that turned into a new encounter of extreme passion. After, they would slip away and go down for breakfast, followed by a short walk through a park near the hotel and a visit to a boutique of antiques and museums. They were just a respite between amalgamations of their bodies, attracted with an uncontrollable force like a magnet to metal. They loved each other fully. Their sparkling eyes, wide smiles, and walks holding hands and embraced; they were seen as owners of the world, walking without touching the ground and exhaling the aroma of sublime love and passion.

The next day they chatted again, the previous conversation had been interrupted when meeting with a friend.

–My dear, please, tell me more about yourself, what has become of your life in the last years? How are your kids? How often do you visit them in Chile, please, tell me.

Todd seemed extremely anxious, dominated by a level of curiosity that made it difficult for him to breathe, intrigued to know more about Esmeralda's life.

–My children are great. They're all grownup, have finished university and are now working; they're successful professionals. I'm very proud of them and I give thanks to God.

–Wow, really? Congratulations! What did they study?

–Apollo is an Engineer, Victoria became a businesswoman, and Renata is an oral surgeon, although after graduating she has dedicated herself more to her passion in music than to her profession, she truly loves music more than being a doctor.

–Congrats once again, they've done a great job, my kids as well: Madeline is a journalist, Anna studied psychology and Johnny is in IT –IT: information technology–. I feel very proud of my children. I love them with all my heart and it's an honour to be their father. They have wonderful lives.

–Yes, indeed, it's amazing how our children are now adults and living a great life; they're independent and forming their own families.

—How often do you travel to Chile to visit your children?

—Two or three times a year, as I have my business in Santiago, I try to travel as much as possible...

—What kind of business?

—I have a dental and beauty clinic.

—Ah, because of Renata?

—Yes, I sold one of my properties to buy a clinic so that she could work independently and at the same time combine work with her passion for music.

—Wonderful, congratulations!

—Yes, however, in my opinion, my daughter hasn't done very well, her priority is still music. She hasn't made any efforts at the clinic and for me it has been a real and great challenge trying to motivate her to go to the clinic and attend to the patients. Being the manager here, from London, isn't easy as dentistry is not my specialty and considering the time difference which is five hours, oh my God, I'm extremely tired and stressed trying to learn about dentistry and facial beauty treatments.

—Oh my dear Esmeralda, as parents we do so much for our kids and unfortunately it's not always well received by them. However, I'm sure she will mature and appreciate everything that you're doing for her...

—Noooo, noooo, she left Chile and is now living in Berlin with her boyfriend who is an artist and a member of a rock band. They're doing super well.

—Well, at least they're doing well with the band.

—Mmhmm, they're starting their music career and as you know, to be a rock star you have to go a long way and they need to be very good to have the opportunity to make their artistic talent known. In fact, I pushed them to do a tour in London; it was wonderful, it was excellent. Anyway, being parents isn't an easy task.

—Tell me about it, I know.

—In short, do you want to get together for coffee?

—I can't tomorrow, I'm sorry. Can we get lunch on Wednesday? —Yes, sounds great, once I finish my English class.

—Ah! You're still studying English?

—Yes, I'm studying professional English so I can get a job as a social worker. Yes, despite being an old woman, I'm still studying and surrounded by young people.

—What? We are not old... just yet, hahaha.

—What are you talking about? I'm even a grandmother.

—Aaaaahhh, so what? You're a grandma? You have grandchildren? Ah, noooo, noooo, I couldn't be more envious. You are extremely lucky to have grandkids.

—Yes, I have three grandchildren.

—Three? I have none. Nooo, nooo, it can't be, it's not fair.

—I'm sorry, I have to go.

—Don't worry; remember we're having lunch together on Wednesday.

—Oh yea, see you Wednesday; but where?

—I'll let you know. I'll look for a nice restaurant near South Kensington.

—Oh, it was wonderful talking to you, mhmm.

—Yes, and there are many, so many and wonderful memories that come to mind, mhmm.

From that day on, Esmeralda couldn't stop smiling, singing and dancing, feeling the closeness and real possibility of seeing and reuniting with her love from the past; a love that had nothing from the past because she relived every moment they spent together and with those moments, the feelings of love and passion took over again. It was a very serious and extremely worrying situation since she was married and loved her husband.

15

She wondered: is it possible to love two men at the same time? Terry is my husband and I love him; however, Todd is unbridled passion that makes my blood boil and my heart race. On the other hand, my husband is calm, tranquil and gives me security; we love each other with our hearts, with serenity... Perhaps it's the British way and with Todd it's the passion of adrenaline, the wild bravery of a cowboy and the passion of a Latin woman, who knows... Stop thinking, you're happily married and Todd is part of your past.

The day of the date she didn't know what to wear, she wanted to look radiant and beautiful like never before, but first she had to attend her classes and she wasn't going to miss them. In short, a beautiful navy blue dress, her magical red shoes and the long golden sand-colored raincoat that wreaked havoc in São Paulo was the outfit she chose, in addition to the pink scarf that gave the finishing touch of delicacy for the encounter with her Sweetheart. She felt unfaithful and guilty betraying her husband; nonetheless, she wondered, and more than anything she justified her actions, saying to herself:

– "I'm not doing anything wrong; we're just going to meet up and talk".

But she knew that nothing could be guaranteed, perhaps everything could flourish again, having been a lapse of twenty years without savoring the honey of the frantic love that united them.

The wait at the station was almost twenty minutes; she was very nervous thinking that maybe she had misheard the name of the station or that he could have had an accident. She walked around the station looking for his face among the passers-by without being able to see him. She returned to her waiting spot, near the exit ticket machines. In that, she sees him approaching with giant steps, his eyes shone like two giant stars in the firmament, smiling nervously and happily at the same time. The strange thing was that he wasn't wearing a suit or tie, as he always did, even outside the office, he was wearing an old baggy and worn-out gray hooded sweatshirt and loose, frayed jeans; he had definitely and completely changed his way of dressing. Another thing that really caught her attention was his height, he looked smaller than she remembered from the image of an intellectual man she had of him, noted for his presence, noble stature and simplicity... In essence and with all that being said, he was her Todd, her Sweetheart. They hugged and greeted each other with great joy, apologizing for his delay:

—It was dumb of me to wait outside the station and not inside–, he even mentioned that he had arrived twenty minutes before, as had she. They laughed, breaking the ice and lowering a bit their level of nervousness.

They started walking towards the restaurant; lunch lasted for more than two hours. It was the first time they had a fluent conversation since Esmeralda had now mastered the English language. They caught up on all the years of absence, focusing on the topic of their children, work and their new lives, making an effort to accept and respect that they had gone their separate ways.

He had been retired for more than six years and was living alone in London near his childhood home, strategically located to be close to his children, although the three had already moved out; only Johnny, the youngest son, lived relatively close to home.

It was time to get up from the table and make way for other diners. He invites her to walk through the beautiful streets of South Kensington and Chelsea, a wonderful area in London and well known for the Flower Show, a festival of flowers, plants, gardens and all things horticultural, organized by the Royal Horticultural Society (RHS), on the grounds of the Royal Hospital Chelsea, home to some 300 retired British Army soldiers known as Chelsea Pensioners, in Chelsea. The RHS is the UK's largest garden charity with about 500,000 members; its purpose being to enrich people's lives through plants and make the UK a greener and prettier country.

Although the Chelsea Flower Show isn't the biggest event of its kind, the accolade goes to the RHS Hampton Court Palace Garden Festival, which is certainly the most famous. It's been dubbed the garden equivalent of Paris Fashion Week or the Gardening World Cup, and it's the highlight of the season when Britons prepare their gardens for summer. The event is something of an English national pastime and is as integrated into the social calendar as Ascot horse races or Henley Royal regattas. That is how each year in May, for five days, the grounds of the Royal Hospital are transformed into a collection of exhibition gardens and a fascinating display of flowers and plants, with hundreds of exhibitors competing for one of the Chelsea Gold Medals. The show is attended by around 160,000 visitors each year, a number limited by the capacity of the venue; tickets must be purchased in advance and usually sell out well before the event. They walked around Sloane Square –Sloane Square is a small garden square situated on the edge of the central London districts of Knightsbridge, Belgravia and Chelsea, 3.4 km southeast of Charing Cross, in Kensington and Chelsea–, an area characterized by the predominance of museums, theaters, cafes and bars, of great tourist affluence and postgraduate students of London College, breathing an atmosphere of art and intoxicating culture. It was an incredible feeling walking next to him. Esmeralda clenched her hands in the pockets of her raincoat, trying to prevent them from escaping in search of Todd's strong and energetic hands; apparently, he was doing the same. It was something so typical of them, walking around holding hands and other times hugging. The magic of love and the light of happiness were perceived even by the butterflies, who today warned of the anguish and uncertainty of the encounter. Evident were the hints of sadness and the fissures of a slow and painful walk, generated by the magnitude of the twenty years that had passed. The gray atmosphere that surrounded them couldn't manage to subside even with the beauty of the gardens, where children laughed chasing the small birds. Old people enjoyed the tenderness of children, and even the ravens and seagulls –typical birds of England–stopped their singing when they saw them pass, and the fox that crossed the corner of Sloane Square also looked at them with pity. Silence accompanied them for most of the walk, as well as sighs and their elusive glances. As they approached the station to begin the return home, Esmeralda said to herself:

–No, no, I can't let him go without telling him how much I still love him, that my love for him has always been in my heart, waiting for him, despite being married to another man and having made a life away from him.

Evidently, both thought the same; they wanted to avoid missing the great opportunity to continue talking and enjoying each other's company. In that, he approaches to give her a kiss on the cheek and say goodbye. She stops him outlining a smile:

–Shall we go to the pub for whisky, please? It's still early –she wasn't capable of confessing how she was dying to hug him passionately and tell him how much she loved him.

20

—Oh yes, let's go get a drink.

At the bar, they both managed to relax and he opened up his heart to her, confessing what he had never told anyone in his life. He talked about his childhood, marked by the physical absence and love from his parents, who used to enjoy gatherings and social events; His mother participated in countless charitable foundations and his father was a senior executive. He and his two brothers were left in the care of nannies days and nights suffering the absence of their parents, especially missing his mother's love. He also commented how painful it was leaving his children, keeping in mind that he cared for them more than their mother, and revealing with deep pain, a very relevant aspect of his family breakup that Esmeralda was unaware of:

—She, the mother of my children, asked me to leave the house when she found out about our relationship. We were living under the same roof, but it had been more than three years since we had stopped sharing a bed. From one night to the next I had nowhere to live, my family had been completely destroyed and my children were devastated; I remember how they cried and begged me not to go. I found a house, much smaller than the family home, a few blocks away, and I bought it, but first I went to live for about six months at a hotel. They were very difficult times, but we could no longer continue living together, our relationship had ended many years before.

He stops to repeat the order of drinks, and when standing up, he surprises her with a kiss on the lips, to which she doesn't respond because he's paralyzed her, despite the fact that she was waiting for it and madly wishing for it to happen. Returning to the table with the two glasses, he kisses her again, and she responds passionately, holding each other's hands, consolidating the reencounter and saying to each other in unison and in silence: "We are never going to separate again, I promise you that. No matter what it takes or what I have to do, our children have grown up and we are getting old depriving ourselves of this great love".

He chugged his glass and continued with the story, his eyes about to burst in a stream of tears. With a rueful voice, he confesses that it was a serious mistake retiring early at the age of 55, without having been prepared for it. He was definitely not ready for that new stage, finding himself alone and with nothing to do. His life became empty and lonely, without having a single person with whom to share, away from his family and with an almost null and terrible relationship with his children. He had become an absent father after the separation, and devoting himself fully to his working life, he found company and comfort in alcohol. He confessed with anger, and furiously hitting the table with the empty glass after finishing the last sip of wine in one gulp:

—I'm a fucking drunk!!

And after tilting the glass once more to savor the last couple of drops of sauvignon blanc, cupping his face with both hands, roughly wiping his tears with his right fist, he stands resolutely for another glass of wine, while Esmeralda opts for passion fruit juice. She was stunned, flabbergasted, trying to assimilate such a painful and unthinkable confession. She refused to believe that about her great love, whom she had admired for his simplicity, elegant distinction, leadership and impeccable and internationally recognized professional career, who had become a leader almost tirelessly due to his busy work schedule that required trips and meetings with presidents of different countries and their ministers. In short, she was astonished, refusing to believe, and even less, accept such cruel information and reality, regretting not having been by his side to take care of him and protect him, and above all, enjoy his love.

Esmeralda gently takes his hands and with compassionate eyes says to him:

—My love, I will take care of you and you will become a healthy man again...

He abruptly interrupts her, although calmer now:

—I'm getting psychiatric and therapeutic treatment; my children are ashamed of me...

He burst into tears. Esmeralda went over and sat next to him, hugged him and contained her deep pain. Seeing a man cry was extremely hard for Esmeralda, since she had grown up in the countryside with a tradition full of prejudices and customs in which one of them was that "men don't cry". In fact, she vividly remembers the only time she saw her father cry, it was in the time before the military coup in Chile, when food and money was scarce as a result of monetary hyperinflation. It was *la hora de onces* —onces: afternoon tea time where Chilean families get together to have tea with a sandwich–, children would complain that they didn't want to drink milk because it tasted bad without sugar, so their mother, even though she managed to arrive early at the Santa Julia shop to stand in line to try and buy as much as she could before they ran out, they couldn't sell her more than half a kilo of sugar allotted per month. No matter how much her mother insisted that she had six children to feed, and although the clerk knew her, she couldn't accede to their mother's cries, since there were dozens of other people waiting in line for groceries to also feed their families. Thank God, the fact that they lived in the countryside was a real privilege compared to families who lived in urban areas. In the countryside it is possible to grow vegetables, raise chickens, ducks and even pigs to feed the family; so her family could never suffer from hunger. Her paternal grandfather was a man who owned large acres of land that her father worked, not only growing potato, corn, wheat, rice and beans, among others,

24

they also raised cattle, sheep and pigs, and had many birds such as chickens, ducks and even peacocks; so they had a large provision. However, they didn't have refined foods such as sugar or oil, which was replaced with lard, nor could they buy flour, so they obtained directly by taking wheat sacks to grind in order to stock up to then make bread.

In this first encounter, Esmeralda went through all the emotional states that there are, nervousness and anxiety in waiting, happiness about their get-together, reliving the abundant love with the surprising kiss, dreaming and being amazed to discover that their love was as intact as the last time they had the pleasure of being together, to finally pass into a state of great concern, compassion and protection towards her beloved Todd when seeing how her Sweetheart melted.

They meet again after two days, and from that gathering, they saw each other daily for a period of three months. After a couple of weeks, he invited her to his house, and even though she wanted with all her soul to go, she was trembling because if she went, she would become an adulterous, which she didn't want because it was against all her principles and values. Sometimes at the end of her class, they would meet up to talk over coffee and a snack, other times they enjoyed an exquisite lunch followed by relaxing and wonderful walks holding hands, something they had always enjoyed. But unfortunately, Esmeralda couldn't see, because she refused to recognize, the obvious signs of alcoholism in which her adorable Sweetheart was submerged.

On the other hand, for Esmeralda it was a great concern and fear running into someone she knew. Living in England for several years now and being the president of Casa Chilena UK for a period of two years, she had become a public person in the Chilean and Latin community, in addition to easily being recognized by Terry's friends for her characteristic and strikingly beautiful shiny black hair that exceeded her thin waist.

Being aware and willing to leave her husband for Todd, there was no longer any reason to wait. The day they decided to meet after school to go to his house, she felt extremely nervous as if it was the first time, they were going to make love. She was shaking so uncontrollably that, getting off at the station near Todd's house, she asked him if they could first stop a bar for drinks because she needed to relax. He understandingly hugged her and led her to a nice bar near his house where they had lunch. The table talk lasted for more than an hour and then they embarked on the path to the culmination of their postponed love.

The house was warm, with large windows that provided a great natural light to the environment, the walls were covered with works of art and a large staircase led to the second level, with shiny parquet flooring. It was a beautiful house but something was missing, the feminine touch of a woman, the fragrance and color of natural flowers, the aroma of food and freshly brewed coffee.

All were excuses that allowed her to postpone the climb up the stairs, until he excitedly hugged her. They kissed passionately and Todd took her in his arms and carried her upstairs. He left her on the bed and they quickly took off their clothes, caressing each other and kissing each other's bodies as they had done in the past, but nothing was the same. Twenty years of absence didn't pass in vain, especially when there's alcoholism and medication for panic attacks and depression. All this contributed to the experience not being what they dreamt, added to the nervousness of giving themselves to each other. The next day was better, a little more pleasant, but for him it was still a matter of great concern and frustration not being able to gracefully respond to Esmeralda's needs. That tormented him and made him drink even more.

She became more and more worried when she noticed Todd's extreme dependence on alcohol and pills; they caused him paranoia, hallucinations, anxiety and panic attacks. Therefore, she decided to take care of him and began a new stage in her life. Every day she got up early and took the train as usual. Her husband thought she was going to English class, but she was on her way to Todd's house, who was waiting for her at the station with a bouquet of flowers, roses or tulips, that she placed everywhere in the house to give it life and the feminine touch it needed.

27

Every time she arrived, he prepared her an exquisite cup of coffee with milk, an aroma that invaded the ground floor of the house. They had lively conversations, laughed, checked their cell phones and then he would take her by the hand and invite her:

—Please, come to bed with me, I'd love for us to cuddle.

And it was literally like that, he would snuggle up next to her, both naked bodies, quickly wrapped around each other and he would fall into a deep sleep, due to the previous night's drunkenness and the mixture of medicines, a dire combination for his health. She would get up with extreme delicacy, trying not to make any noise so as not to interrupt his sleep, she would go downstairs to the kitchen to clean, wash the dishes and throw away the three or four empty bottles of wine that he had drunk the night before. In the moments in which he seemed to be a bit more sober and lucid, she would ask him to please not drink as much, that it wasn't healthy and even worse that it kept him away from his children. Of course, he tried, but being plunged into a deep depression it was almost impossible. Esmeralda made an effort to take care of him, but it was very difficult not being with him at night, a critical moment because he drank nonstop and without witnesses. He would even get up in the middle of the night just to buy more alcohol, take a glass and a bottle to bed, and every time he woke up, he would take a few sips of wine.

28

Esmeralda completely changed her behavior, she stopped calling and messaging her husband as she used to do every day, she no longer waited for him with eagerness, and she stopped accompanying him to his activities, giving him free rein to do as he pleased, not caring about where he went, who he met and what time he returned. She even stopped accompanying him to rock concerts and gigs, appearing happy and radiant, becoming the most accommodating and idyllic wife. However, when it came to getting to the marital bed... there was always an excuse to avoid having sex; she would go to bed before him or very late, making sure he was asleep. She acted tired and at times even pretended to be sick, being sporadic the nights in which she had to give in to the sexual requirements of her husband, and when faced with the urgent need to fulfill her conjugal duty, she gave herself with overflowing passion, self-convinced in body, soul and heart that she was merging in a fiery night of passion with her beloved Todd; She even involuntarily said his name at the moment of orgasm. Realizing and wanting to pronounce his name, she repeated it tirelessly with a very soft and unintelligible voice, feeling fully and absolutely satisfied.

They began to plan their life together. Todd begged her every time she visited him not to leave, to stay, to move in with him, and she wanted to with all her heart. However, it was due to her husband, to whom she was united by strong feelings of love, respect and gratitude; although nothing compared to her beloved Todd, whom was also no longer the same. Every day he looked more deteriorated, aged, haggard, tired and weak, and in silence she cried inconsolably when seeing her Sweetheart was melting.

Even from the beginning, she had always been on board with the idea of living together, but begged him to give her time so she could talk with Terry; she needed to find the most appropriate moment to talk about such a delicate matter.

She carefully took care of him, preparing food for him, encouraging him to walk, sunbathe, and even go out just to get some fresh air. Weekends were terrible, because they couldn't see each other and he drank a lot more than usual. She would send him WhatsApp messages giving him daily tasks: "You have to get out of bed", "Have your cereal and milk", "Go for a walk, even if it's 15 minutes", "Prepare yourself something to eat", "Take a bath", and "Avoid drinking alcohol". Every day she called him and messaged him to make sure that he was alright, that he had gotten up, that he had had breakfast… but he drank too much and even tried to hide the evidence. Despite this, every day she found three or four empty bottles of wine, although he hid them or threw them away, the traces of his excessive alcohol consumption the night before were evident. He didn't eat, he only had cereal and milk for breakfast, just like a child, which he repeated in the afternoon or when he felt hungry or remembered that he had to eat, in addition to the fact that he couldn't always do so because he didn't have food, his refrigerator and pantry were always empty, and it wasn't because he didn't have money. He had abandoned his hygiene habits, he didn't brush his teeth and not to mention taking a bath, he even smelled bad.

Todd began to get worse, to have hallucinations, delusions of persecution. He saw people and heard voices, sometimes he called her at night or in the wee hours of the morning asking for help, to please call the police because intruders had entered his house and were hiding, that he could hear them without being able to see them… His voice was terrifying, of panic and of absolute and complete fear, managing to infect poor Esmeralda, who found herself with her hands tied.

And apart from all that, he began to have problems with the neighbors, who complained about the disturbing noises he made at night and because he filled their garbage cans with his own trash. When Esmeralda decides to go live with her Sweetheart, she asks him to get rid of Maria's belongings, a Brazilian woman he had met online and had lived with for almost two years; Esmeralda had found some woman's clothing and personal items in the house. He admitted to her that he had had a sporadic relationship with a woman, who had been very cruel to him and that was why they had broken up, that she was a liar and a bad person, who had deeply hurt him and destroyed his life. He spoke about her with so much rage and fury, to the point that it seemed like flames were going to come out of his eyes and mouth. That situation was worrying and very uncomfortable for Esmeralda, since he used to call her Maria and not Esmeralda, and no matter how much she insisted that she was Esmeralda, he always said the other name. She even put a name tag on her lapel and left several others in different places of the house, including the kitchen, bathroom and obviously, in the bedroom, but despite that he kept calling her Maria; although it ended up being an excellent strategy.

One morning, he didn't show up at the station to pick her up, and when she got home, he opened the door completely naked and shivering with cold, gave her a furtive good-morning kiss and quickly went upstairs to his room. Esmeralda was shocked to see the difficulty with which he moved and the large number of bruises that covered his back, buttocks and legs. She saw blood scattered on the floor, on the stairs and towards the bathroom and kitchen. She placed her hands on her face and thanked God for finding him alive, and without knowing what had happened the night before, she followed him to the bedroom where he had wrapped himself up as well as he could, quivering with a fever; he asked her to cuddle next to him and keep him warm; Esmeralda did it just like every day, and in this occasion, it was like a mother protecting her child or an unconditional friend. He clung to her with trembling strength in search of warmth and protection. The cold pierced Esmeralda, who also began to tremble, but in her case, it was more of terror than cold given the urgent need to know what had happened to him the night before and in particular, the origin of the blood.

Unable to get away from him to find out, she tried to get information out of him, but he only replied that he was cold, to hug him and cover his body with more blankets. As soon as it was possible, she got out of bed with a stealthy step, fearing that she would discover something she didn't want to be true, that intruders had indeed entered the house and a violent fight had broken out; she decided to inspect the house. There was evidence of blood scattered across the floor and bloody footprints clearly marked in the direction of the bedroom, the bathroom and the kitchen, but not towards the exit door. With great terror, she grabbed one of her magical red shoes and took courage to find out what had happened, afraid of facing some delinquent still inside the house. She didn't find anyone in the adjoining room, but she did find an open red suitcase with woman's clothing; a couple of those big push-up bras that simulate more bust caught her attention and she also found pink colored patent leather heels. The impression she had was that the owner of the clothing wasn't a decent woman, but instead one of those who had sex for money.

Cautiously, she went down the stairs barefoot and in that she felt that something was embedded in one of her feet. It was a thick piece of glass, apparently from a glass or a bottle, which tore the sock but didn't manage to seriously injure her foot. It did make a slight cut that began to bleed, making the crime scene even more baleful, a crime that she still couldn't decipher, although she had just discovered that there was a woman involved...

When she got to the ground floor of the house, she realized that the coffee table was a shattered; there were empty wine bottles on the floor, papers, telephone cables, chargers and Todd's cell phone completely dead. She tiptoed so as not to make any noise or hurt her foot even more. She didn't see anyone in the living room, but as she approached the kitchen the amount of blood increased and the trembling in her legs immobilized her; seized by fear she again took courage to continue. She tried to stay strong, there was only one room left to check and that was where she would surely find answers. She drew strength from weakness and took the largest knife she found in the kitchen, leaving the high heel shoe on the messy countertop along with glasses and unwashed dishes.

The traces of blood going to the bathroom were more intense; the door was ajar and she tried to see without opening it, but since she couldn't, she kicked it hard and it opened wide. There was even more blood and more traces on the floor, towels soaked mostly by blood than water; the scene was frightening, but she found no one. She breathed easier, although still frozen with fear since she yet had to check the second floor and the attic. She gathered courage and wielding the knife, tiptoed up the stairs, checked on Todd, who was sleeping soundly with legs trembling and shivering; it was a mixture of the low temperatures of the cold autumn and the beginning of the harsh English winter. But the chattering of her teeth and the shivering of her small body was the terrifying fear, not the cold.

Upon reaching the top floor of the house, the scene before her eyes was woman's clothing and accessories scattered throughout the room and on the bed. The attic door was open, there was a baleful darkness inside and fear paralyzed her. Drawing strength from weakness and dagger in hand, she managed to ask in a strong and determined tone:

–Who's there? Come out immediately or I'll call the police. I'm warning you; I'm armed and you won't get away from here alive – a hollow silence was the only response. She insists with a firmer and more threatening voice:

–Come out or I'll call the police; it's up to you–nothing, everything was absolutely silent.

–I'm warning you that you're not going to leave here alive, don't play hard to get. Te police are about to arrive, I called them before coming up –she sat and waited, her knuckles white from pressuring down on the knife handle, she was alert and willing to stab the weapon as many times as necessary.

After about five minutes, she decided to peak through the attic hatch; with her cell-phone's flashlight she managed to see inside. The attic was small, with a height of no more than a meter at the highest point and rectangular in shape, ending in zero. She followed the shape of the roof; there was no intruder, just bags and boxes piled one on top of the other, an absolute mess, some damaged and others empty, torn and open, you could see woman's shoes and clothing as well as household items and decorations; by now it was clear that they were Maria's belongings, the girl who used to live with Todd. But that wasn't the relevant thing; the important thing was to find out where all that blood had come from and know how many people had been involved.

Calmer knowing that there wasn't an intruder in the house, she went downstairs to make sure the front door was closed; she locked it and ran to snuggle up next to Todd. She hugged him looking for security, to lower her anxiety, her fear and to keep warm; between dreams, he hugged her and pressed against her body. After relaxing a bit, she carefully got up and took the phone, which was absolutely dead, plugged it in, and as soon as she was able to turn it back on, she began to search for information, trying to find out what might have happened the night before.

36

She found endless messages similar to the ones he had sent her; he had also messaged his journalist friend, Elizabeth, and another friend from Chicago, telling them that intruders had broken into his home that they wanted to kill him, that they were talking to him and he couldn't see them because they were hiding from him; he said he was very afraid, and asked them to please call the police. She also found extensive and melodramatic messages of reproach to Maria, who had left him at the beginning of October, alluding that it was terrible living with him, that he was untrustworthy, that he didn't acknowledge her and that he had a drinking problem. Maria complained that he didn't present her as his girlfriend, that he denied their relationship to his friends; she also mentioned the almost null relationship with his children, and how he instead criticized her for communicating daily with his daughter Rebecca. They talked about the difficult and traumatic moments experienced as a result of the Maria's father dying in Todd's arms. They also remembered a day when it was pouring rain and he picked her up at the train station and took her home. He also reproached her for the time Maria's family visited them in London and he had cooked for them every day without her spending a dime, which was all coming from his pockets. In a nutshell, they were all reproaches of bad taste; he even demanded that she return the engagement ring. In that, she hears Todd coming down the stairs. Quickly and before being discovered, she leaves the phone on the floor and gets up to help him down; he looked haggard, battered and was limping. She helped him sit on his sofa, where he spent days, hours and nights with his tablet and cell phone in hand reading and writing, with a glass on the table and a couple of bottles of wine on the side of the chair, usually empty.

After sitting down, he raises his right foot showing and asking Esmeralda to check the wound. It was an open, deep wound, still with fresh blood. Shocked, she asks what happened:

—Last night when those intruders entered the house, trying to get away so they wouldn't kill me, I tripped over the coffee table, fell on it and it broke into a thousand pieces, along with a couple of glasses and bottles of wine. It was dark because they had turned off the light so that I wouldn't identify them, and when I tried to run, to avoid being killed, I stepped on a piece of glass causing this tremendous wound; I also have another on my back and here on my arm.

Esmeralda is dumbfounded listening to the story, trying to tie up loose ends and putting the story together. However, how did the intruders escape? What were they looking for? Todd most likely attacked them; they must have left wounded. Will they come back? It was a whirlwind of questions. She sighed deeply and managed only to say:

—Thank God you're alive; luckily, they didn't harm you.

—Yes, luckily, I managed to get away from them. But look, they're still in the house, can't you hear them? I can hear them, they're talking, they're coming, and they're going to kill us. Call the police, now. Please, don't let them kill me, please, please. Can't you see them? There they are. They're two of them, no, they're three. There's another one. There are several of them. I can't see them, they're hiding again; I can only hear them...

Esmeralda realizes that he isn't well; he apparently seems to be having hallucinations, delusions, seeing and hearing imaginary voices. She asks him to calm down, telling him that she will defend him, that she has just called the police and that they're on their way, that they will arrive soon, and that the ambulance will take him to the hospital to treat his wounds. He refuses to go to the hospital, but is glad to know that the police are on their way...

Together with Elizabeth, without communicating directly, and both using their strategies independently, they manage to convince him to go to the hospital. Elizabeth tells him, step by step, the procedures, being truthful in the information and even aggravating the symptoms in order to obtain urgent medical care. They agree to meet at a train station near the medical service where Elizabeth would pick him up in her car to take him —Esmeralda would eventually discover that Elizabeth was still romantically interested in him—. Upon learning that he was with Esmeralda, who was also accompanying him, she reacted furiously, asking who she thought

39

she was assisting him without knowing anything about his medical history or previous treatment; her anger and jealousy led her to desert. Todd reacted angrily commenting that her attitude wasn't from a person who was his so called friend, that it was strange and disappointing. He took his jacket, tightly grabbed Esmeralda by the hand and they started towards the train station, located three blocks from the house. The chilly autumn morning sank into their bones, despite the sun which shone without keeping warm; they walked quickly, their faces reddened from the cold and feeling discomfort in their nose, ears and cheeks. He continued to complain about the lack of help and consideration from his friend, it had clearly affected and disappointed him. In the past she had helped him by calling the emergency health service, getting him hospitalized and receiving effective and timely treatment in crisis situations due to the excessive intake of alcohol mixed with medications from his psychiatric treatment, which severely took a toll on his health, not to mention the chaos in self-medicating, taking two or three times the dose or forgetting to do so, in addition to the sleeping pills.

When they arrived at the hospital, he immediately received medical attention; he was very clear and precise in his answers. He told them about the hallucinations, the lack of sleep and excessive alcohol consumption. He was quickly referred to a psychiatrist, who carried out the anamnesis, admitting him to the hospital.

Esmeralda never left his side; her presence gave him security and tranquility. During that visit to the doctor, Esmeralda learned unpublished passages from the life of her beloved Todd; she was surprised, stunned, amazed, she saw him so fragile. It moved her to the core and provoked feelings of deep compassion, a trigger that had pushed her to make the decision of abandoning her 21st century prince in order to dedicate herself fully and completely to the care of her true love, her Sweetheart. She felt the urgent need to win him back. She regretted not having been with him during his previous crises, and it would have been better if they had never separated, consummating their great love and passion, thus avoiding the deplorable state he had reached. He confessed that his children felt ashamed to see that he had become an alcoholic and obese, destroying his life; His heaviest weight had been more than one hundred and twenty kilograms, regaining his normal weight after severe hours at the gym and with a strict diet from a professional specialist.

He remembers how one day he was very ill, lying on the floor and vomiting blood. His children and their mother tried to help him, but he wouldn't listen to them, his obstinacy and stubbornness surpassed any hint of sanity, and when he had it, he called Elizabeth who saved him from death. He was hospitalized, received detox treatment and rehabilitation therapy for alcoholism. They were months in which he lost weight and reflected on his life; regretting having retired too soon, not being ready for a life without a clear goal. He longed to travel the world, but he found himself alone and without anyone, and having no company and being so dependent on other people, because during his working life everything had been done for him by his subordinates, including the payment of his personal bills and his laundry, he found that alcohol had become his faithful and inseparable friend, and it was in those moments that he wrote a short and decisive email to Esmeralda:

—I'm ready to go and live with you in Chile!!!

Esmeralda, who had waited so many years for that much-anticipated declaration of love, received the message at the least opportune moment, the day before her marriage, when everything was ready and set to begin her life with another man, whom she also loved. However, Todd was everything and more, and as an empowered woman, she took a deep breath, deleted the message and blocked the email, closing all possibility of contact and ending one of the most important chapters of her love life.

When relating to the psychiatrist his stormy life as an alcoholic, product of facing loneliness, without work, without purpose, he clung to the only company he had: alcohol, and being malnourished and not exercising, it quickly transformed him into an obese and addicted man, messy and unconcerned about his health. His stories were of profound, deep pain and self-pity, at

42

times turning into anger against himself, into rage and frustration. He clung tightly to Esmeralda's hand. She remained seated on one side of the stretcher, while on the other side was the psychiatrist, who took his time carrying out the anamnesis, looking at the patient with wisdom and tenderness, without departing from his professionalism; from time to time, he would subtly glance at Esmeralda.

Once the anamnesis was finished, the doctor asked if he wanted to add anything else.

–No, nothing – Todd responded.

–And you, do you wish to add anything, ma'am?

She, with a look of love and infinite sweetness, still clinging on to her beloved's hand, asked him in a tone of plea:

–May I?

–Yes, of course, please!

She began by thanking the excellent medical attention Todd had received and that she was happy he had finally sought out professional help. After that brief introduction, she turned her gaze at the patient, and with a sweet soft voice began to say:

–Doctor, the patient who lies on this stretcher isn't even the shadow of that healthy, active and brilliant professional I once knew; I trust that he will recover thanks to your intervention, to

43

his fundamental willpower, and to all the support, care and love that I give him. I would like to add that in reality, he sometimes drinks more than two or three bottles, although you have to subtract the drinks that I have. Another thing that really worries me are his hallucinations, he tells me that he sees people and hears voices, that they want to attack him; he feels scared and asks to call the police. The other issue is that he doesn't sleep well, he suffers from nightmares and talks in his sleep; well actually, it isn't so much talking as it's fighting with fury and rage.

Todd agrees with her comments adding and ratifying the information, indicating that everything is due to the change of medication and the sleeping pills he bought online, that before starting the new treatment indicated by the psychiatrist, he was fine, that he didn't have hallucinations, delusions, or anxiety or panic attacks.

He was hospitalized so they could run more tests and start treatment depending on the results. He gave her the keys to his house so that she could go and get him a change of clothes, pajamas and toiletries.

The next morning, upon returning to the hospital, she was surprised to find him in the reception area. Yes, he had been discharged, the tests had been done the night before and everything was normal. They changed his medication and discharged him with an appointment to see a therapist for alcohol detoxification. Apparently, medicine in the UK is known for trying to avoid hospitalizations by performing most procedures on an outpatient basis.

He returned home more relieved, smiling and happy. Esmeralda decided to go to the supermarket to buy food, vegetables and fruits, and when he put a couple of bottles of wine in the shopping cart, he promised her that he would be very careful with his drinking, that he would be prudent. In fact, he wrote her a letter with promises to keep, including not drinking more than two bottles of wine a day, going for a walk, going to the gym, communicating more often with his children, respecting her and taking care of her. He begged her to go live with him, that it was time and that he needed her.

Esmeralda agreed to move in with him, considering that it was the right time and confident that with her care he would recover again, and they would consecrate their love. She had eagerly prepared for that long-awaited moment, the beginning of a life with her great and true passion; she had no doubt about her love and about ending things with her husband to go live with Todd. Of course, it hurt her deeply to leave Terry, despite the differences they were united by love, a serene and mature love of mutual respect, which she put an end to with a single and accurate blow, a blow that he never expected or imagined, because he loved her so much and saw her so happy, relaxed and condescending, believing that their marriage had consolidated, matured and settled. He was absolutely unaware that the freedom, the lack of reproaches and the trust shown was due to her determination to end the marriage. Esmeralda stopped reproaching his frequent outings to rock concerts, his late arrivals, the excess of beers he drank, in her opinion, hanging out and drinking with his after playing tennis; in short, not even the strong smell of curry annoyed her. Meanwhile, he was completely unaware that Esmeralda's wardrobes and drawers were basically empty, she had gotten rid of a lot of clothes and shoes that she didn't wear and of the garments that she had repeated by dozens, such as her excessive desire to collect raincoats, shoes and handbags. There were endless trips to charitable foundations to donate bags filled with her belongings, as well as books and decorative items.

Esmeralda continued to be stunned and grateful for the incredible opportunity of accompanying him to the hospital, allowing her to discover episodes of his life that she would have never imagined; episodes regarding the difficulties he faced after the separation and not being able to freely see his children; he only saw them once every fortnight and two weeks during summer vacation. He talked about the resounding way in which he gained weight, weighing more than a hundred kilograms, at the same time that he became an alcoholic. Both events took place during his first year of unplanned retirement, although he longed for it, with countless plans that became unattainable dreams when he found himself completely isolated and unable to enjoy and travel the world alone, and not accompanied as he had planned. A close work subordinate suggested him, before retiring, to register on an online page to find friends and a girlfriend to accompany him during his new stage of life. That was how he met the Australian, whom he described as a very beautiful model he lived with for a couple of years until she immediately broke off the relationship, forcing him to leave her house. She had read the email he had written to Esmeralda the day they met for the first time in London; during the time she traveled to study English. The email was a true love letter written from the depths of his heart, describing in extreme detail Esmeralda's face and dazzling beauty, her transparent and naive gaze, possessing the most beautiful smile he had ever seen in his life, the great joy she had in being able to communicate despite her very poor English; however, their body language and the magic of love allowed them to communicate perfectly. That is how he declared his love to her. He also wrote about how stupid he had been in letting her go and not marrying her, that his love, feelings and intoxicating passion were still intact, and had even increased with their encounter, feeling their reciprocity and the desire to relive everything they experienced and enjoyed on their travels, giving a brief description of them.

Esmeralda was on cloud nine and the Australian had taken the bull by the horns, literally throwing him onto the street. Accompanying him to the hospital also allowed her to learn more about Elizabeth, the journalist, whom he met through Twin Souls without bearing any love relationship, but rather a friendship. She was a strong-willed, intellectual and dominant Irish woman, with a pretty face, although he didn't like her smell and her belly. Ah! Elizabeth knew of the intense relationship he had had with Esmeralda, and it gave her hives just hearing her name. And the famous Maria, who apparently entered his life at the moment he most needed a pious soul, generating a very strong relationship, although becoming sick and toxic due to their constant arguments because of Maria's jealousy when learning about Elizabeth, with whom Todd communicated daily and saw from time to time. Added to all that was the alcoholism and envy at seeing how close she was to his daughter and family, relationship and family affections that he lacked, being raised by nannies in the absence of his parents who were a couple of diplomats with an agenda full of social commitments. In full, both the psychiatrist who received him in the emergency room and carried out the anamnesis to determine the seriousness of his illness and requiring hospitalization, as well as the treating physician, had scrutinized very deep and transcendent passages of his life, searching for triggering psychological factors of depression, anxiety and alcoholism.

Loneliness, social distancing and the absence of a close and affective relationship with his children, led him to create and imagine long-awaited for situations, such a birthday in the bosom of a traditional family; He had even made Esmeralda believe that a couple of huge packages received a week before his birthday, that were still unopened, were gifts from his daughters who had apparently sent him a couple of beautiful paintings, bearing in mind that their father had a refined taste for art; hallucinations that vanished when Esmeralda read that the sender was the workshop where he had sent a couple of paintings by an American photographer whom he admired to be framed. In the same way, he reproached the existence of mothers, like Maria, who communicated daily with their children, considering it an extreme and unhealthy dependency.

Esmeralda, after reading his WhatsApp daily, got to know Todd and felt sorry for him and even more so when she saw him cry inconsolably because of the almost null relationship with his children, and in particular with Anna, his favorite daughter, who reproached him for his attitude and completely ignored his existence. He spent days and nights sitting on the sofa with his eyes lost in infinity, scratching his head, he did that so much that he had lost some hair on the upper part of his scalp, to which he commented with joy and pride that his daughter Anna did the same, that she had copied from him that eagerness to scratch her head on the crown... That was how Esmeralda induced him to stop writing those long and endless messages and emails, rebuking them for their behavior, complaining and lamenting one and a thousand incidents, messages that a teenager never reads because of its length and because they know that they're repetitive events that will continue to occur. At first, he refused to listen, responding that it wasn't his way of communicating and that it didn't seem appropriate, however, after a couple of weeks he began to smile and comment that his daughter Madeleine, and even Anna, had written back, letting him know that they were doing very well and working and that one of them even had a boyfriend. He would never admit that he had followed Esmeralda's advice. He wrote to his friend from Chicago mentioning that the relationship with his daughters was prospering and all thanks to the brilliant idea of sending short messages, with a brief greeting and saying goodbye with love; that he was no longer speaking of past quarrels.

Alberto, the neighbor that lived in the basement located on the ground floor, frequently complained about Todd's poor living, prior to Esmeralda's arrival, complaining that he made too much noise during the day and night, that he threw garbage in front of the house and filled up not only his but the neighbor's garbage cans. These events had a snowball effect that escalated one morning when they were cleaning and Todd swept mold and moss from the rooftop that had grown during the winter, falling on the terrace table in the patio where Alberto's wife was, who was savoring an aromatic Italian coffee while talking on the phone with her mother in Spain; a call that was noisily interrupted by the leaves and moss that fell on her coffee cup and her body. It was waste accumulated on the small roof of the balcony overlooking the garden, product of the humidity generated by the rains and the dust, which Todd swept without the slightest care or taking the time to look if there was anyone in the patio, literally throwing the trash on his neighbor's head and into her coffee cup. Sofia's anger was such that she screamed about her upstairs neighbor's horrific behavior:

–This is unheard of, once again throwing your garbage on my terrace and garden, and now in my coffee and on my head. I will call the police. You're unbearable and you're filthy.

He responded angrily, ignoring his neighbor's complaints and urging her to even call the pope if she really wanted to. The argument lasted about five minutes, with mutual verbal aggression and zero respect, without admitting or acknowledging his fault, and pointing out that it was just a little mold, that it wouldn't harm her garden at all.

The next day, Todd didn't open the door for Esmeralda, despite her insistence to the point of almost knocking it down. Her extreme concern led her to his neighbor's house on the ground floor for possible information. Alberto introduced himself receiving her with great kindness and eager to have the opportunity to talk with her; he told her that he had seen him leave in the middle of the afternoon and come back, and that he had been calm without making any disturbing noises. Esmeralda thanked him for the information and introduced herself as Todd's friend and social worker, who visited him daily because she was very concerned about his health. Alberto commented in detail about his neighbor's terrible behavior, classifying him as an awful and demented person. That is how she found out about the previous unpleasant episodes and delved into who Maria was and her relationship with Todd. Esmeralda was stunned; her idol was crumbling into pieces, as hard as she tried to retain the integrity of the image of an intellectual and kind gentleman and, above all, a very thoughtful person towards others, the community and the environment, since obviously he worked in charitable organizations worldwide. She made every effort to apologize on his behalf, commenting that he wasn't in good health, that he was suffering from severe depression and undergoing psychiatric treatment.

Esmeralda understood that Maria had left with only what fit in a suitcase, likewise she ignored the fact that Todd was an expert in hiding evidence of his past relationships, alluding that he was a reserved person and as such, didn't want to share his personal or family life and even less his love life with friends and acquaintances. After some time and new life experiences with him, it would be revealed that he would use his girlfriends, in the first place, in search of company, security and with whom to talk, eat and drink, in addition to cleaning and maintaining the household; it could be said that he was ashamed of them, treating them as mere acquaintances in front of the neighborhood, family and friends. She remembers how one day on their way to an antique store, located a few blocks from his home, they were going to buy a desk for him to use at the dental clinic; before reaching the premises, he released her hand and in a firm tone ordered:

–Don't hold my hand especially when we're out shopping, because the owner, that man over there, is an acquaintance of my children's mother.

–So, who cares? She is no longer your spouse, I am.

–Yes, but I don't want him to find out, and least of all her.

–But, why? I don't understand…

He interrupts her, and abruptly and in a demanding tone, orders her to shut up saying:

–Because I say so, period!

Thus began the road to ruin. The veil that had concealed for more than twenty years a blind and idealistic love, a fantasy made reality by a woman madly in love, naive and dreamy, who would give everything just for love, began to fall. Denial that repeated in his telephone conversations with Elizabeth, lamenting the loneliness and abandonment, the eternal days of waiting for a call, a message from his children, of Christmases, New Years and birthdays in absolute solitude, an absolute lie, not like the absence of his children. He had been spent the previous two years celebrating with Maria and her family, and the new festivities were now being celebrated with Esmeralda, who made an effort to make him feel happy by going out of her way with attention, gifts, company, excessive love and a burning passion like a volcano, waiting for his improvement in order to quench that boiling lava and surrender to the lust and pleasure that had united them since their first encounter after meeting in Santiago, Chile.

He is an expert in hiding even the slightest details, any evidence that could reveal the existence or presence of another living being in his life and in his home. He got rid of all of Maria's belongings before starting a life together with Esmeralda. He wanted to erase a very recent past, denying its existence with the sole fact of eliminating all material evidence. That was how the neighbor's garbage cans, of the adjoining houses and of the front, were filled and overflowing with women's clothing, books, handbags, household items, decorations, even photographs. In short, it was quite a bit of stuff; he threw out suitcases, even the bedding and a couple of pieces of furniture on the corner next to a small square. Along the way, a trail of shoes, earrings and even a pair of bras were left behind; literally tossing on the street all the belongings of a woman he had once promised marriage. –In England it is customary to leave various articles and even unused furniture outside the house available to anyone who wants to take it, all absolutely free and in good condition. –

The neighbors reacted furiously and extremely bothered. It was a bad habit that had dragged on for several years, filling the neighbors' garbage cans with everything he needed to get rid of, including construction material. One Sunday at mid-morning, when Esmeralda had just arrived, a couple of neighbors knocked on the door of his house to complain about his bad behavior. He responded aggressively and loudly, calling them trash and the worst neighbors he had ever had in his entire life, without admitting that he was the person who generated discomfort and problems in the neighborhood; between screams, they threatened to call the police and even got into a fist fight.

It wasn't long before a certified letter arrived from the local municipality, with a large fine he had to pay for disobeying the law and for violating the good coexistence and order of the neighborhood, backing it up with photographs of piles of garbage piled on the street and in the neighbors' dumpsters; even in a couple of them Todd appeared throwing bags full of clothes in the

garbage cans –Poor Maria's belongings would now become trash–
, a fact that Esmeralda would have experienced, but fortunately
avoided with the end of the confinement order from the English
government as a result of the Coronavirus pandemic. However,
Esmeralda was aware that Todd's mental disorders prevented him
from having sanity and respecting the canons of good conduct,
with a high probability of repeating the events unceremoniously
and effortlessly after the previous experience.

Todd declared himself a reserved person, reticent about
sharing his personal life, even with his close friends and
acquaintances, former work colleagues and university pals,
residents of Chicago, the city where he had been born, raised and
studied; he was a brilliant Harvard student. They were his only
friends, apart from Elizabeth, with whom he had now formed a
friendship based on the discussion of news events fed by her in
her capacity as a journalist for a leading newspaper in the United
Kingdom; she had also opened the doors for Madeleine to begin
her career in the journalistic world, a gesture he would always be
grateful for. In essence, more than reserved, he was known for his
double standard with his girlfriends. There were at least four
women in his life, the Australian model being one of them with
whom he lived for a couple of years and abruptly broke up after
reading that wonderful email Todd had written to Esmeralda; Any
person, in their right mind, endowed with self-love and high self-

esteem, solvency, security and independence, who reads a message of such intensity and frenzy, breaks off the relationship immediately, as the Australian did. Regarding that episode, he would constantly complain and reproach Esmeralda that he broke up with that woman because of her, and did the same later on with Maria. He was characterized for never recognizing his faults, his errors and bad behavior, holding others accountable and classifying them as bad people that have destroyed his life.

Another one of Todd's girlfriends was Elizabeth, and finally Maria, a young Brazilian who came into his life at the perfect moment, when he was finishing his anti-alcoholic therapy and had the psychological strategies and tools to redirect his life on a path of future goals and well-being. He clung to her with all his might, transforming her into his salvation, completely giving themselves to one another and living their relationship with frenzy. She, a single mother of a teenager, who lacked love and protection, found it easy to cling to and surrender herself entirely to this new possibility of life. Both at home and constantly together, she jobless and he retired, their relationship became suffocating and rocky; Dominated by insecurities, jealousy and absurd arguments, he went back to excessively drinking alcohol, although he promised again and again that he would stop. Before their failed relationship, they traveled to Brazil for six months, to Maria's parent's house, where he was received with open arms by the whole family, and in particular by her father, who was sick and who saw in him the perfect partner for his daughter, with whom he could marry her off and die in peace. They spent entire afternoons together, Todd and Maria's father, playing card games, learning fun facts and interesting stories of their youth, work and family, laughing out loud, and he had even planned to acquire a piece of land adjoining the property to build a house for him and Maria; a Christmas with the family being the occasion he took advantage of to give her an engagement ring. Then, her father's deteriorated health worsened; they accompanied him days and nights by his hospital bed, until he died in Todd's arms, an event that would mark a before and after in his life.

Upon returning to London, the arguments intensified and once again alcohol had gotten the better of him. Then, Maria moved to her sister's house in Switzerland, who had been diagnosed with cancer and was unable to care for her young son who was just a year old. She left at the beginning of October after a strong argument, and bearing in mind her sister's call for help, she left that house with no desire to return. It was during that time that Esmeralda contacted Todd, completely unaware that he had just ended a relationship and was in full mourning, a fact that would be disastrous in their reencounter.

Todd had made Esmeralda promise that they would spend the day and night of his birthday together, being such a special day and in the state of loneliness and crisis that invaded him, it was the least she could do. Faced with the obstacle of how she would spend the night away from home, she trembled looking for the best and unsuspicious excuse that wouldn't cause the slightest doubt; she found it. She left the house alluding that she was going to visit a friend who needed her support because she wasn't feeling well and would supposedly spend the whole day with her. She called Terry two or three times during the day, letting him know the seriousness of her friend's health, which had aggravated to such a point that she had called an ambulance; after having waited more than three long hours and some more between medical attention and tests, it was early morning and since the train stations were closed, it was impossible to return home, so she would stay to take care of her friend, besides her cell phone had died… It was the first time she slept away from home. She was caught between two strong currents of feelings generated by the love of two men, both deserving of all her love and to share a life together. One was a vivid and latent memory, at least in her heart, of a past of euphoric love and passion, with the burning desire to be and feel like a woman; it was like being born again. The other, his contender, was calm and serene, like the moment of ease of the world's most troubled river. "What should I do?" was the question that tormented her. Finally, her heart of sweetness and infinite mercy chose to take care of her fragile and tormented Todd, without imagining that such decision would lead her to live the cold proximity of death and desolation.

Very carefully and in advance, she planned his birthday party which would be intimate, just the two of them. She bought an exquisite chocolate cake, his favorite, champagne, an excellent bottle of Chilean wine, decorations for the house, a few gifts and even crystal glasses. The kitchen only had the basics, there wasn't special tableware for celebrations or at least of good taste, just as Esmeralda was used to, buying glasses, trays and plates to share delicacies. Todd tells her that they would have lunch with Johnny, his son, a fact that makes her euphoric with happiness, finally feeling that he was going to integrate her into his family. He had entrusted her with a key to the house, so that morning she arrived earlier than usual, sneaked in, avoiding making the slightest noise, and decorated the living room with streamers, balloons and fresh flowers of exquisite fragrance, giving luminosity to the room on that cloudy and cold autumn day in mid-October. Once everything was ready, she went up to the bedroom, took off her clothes and gently slipped into bed, hungry for passion and love, wanting to make this awakening an unforgettable birthday; the atmosphere felt more pleasant as the temperature increased after turning on the heater and slowly dissipating the cold of the night and the dew of dawn. She began the ceremony of love with a soft and warm kiss on the neck while she brought her body closer and closer to his, feeling and caressing his body was true ecstasy; her breathing becoming agitated just knowing she was next to her Sweetheart. He responded with a soft moan, at the same time that he tightly snuggled her close to his body as if preventing her from escaping. She, more aroused than ever, tried to free herself from those heavy arms in search of passion and lust, but no matter how hard she tried it was impossible, he was still under the influence of alcohol and medicine. He seemed to be in a daze, to which she gave in and snuggled, passing from the arms of Venus to those of Morpheus; it was like every day she visited him, regardless of whether it was morning or afternoon. He was used to taking her by the hand with a look of mischief and sparkle in his eyes, leading her upstairs to his room, quickly taking off all his clothes, and inviting her to cuddle up next to him, both naked, enjoying the tenderness and the warmth of their bodies; relaxed, serene, he more than her. Uncontrolled passion burned in her veins and alcohol in his which lulled him to sleep, distancing him more each day from the virility and carnal enjoyment that had united them in a distant past. After resting for a few minutes, she became restless, wanting to relive the passion of love, refusing to recognize and accept that there was nothing left but the memory and languid sighs of nostalgia of that pleasure; no matter how hard she tried and resorted to the daring and lustful deliveries that had made them moan with satisfaction and love, regardless of the time or anything, the intoxication of love had been transformed into intoxication of alcohol and pills, annihilating all hint of sensuality. He could take two or even three Viagra pills in search of an erection, reaching an illusory virility that would quickly vanish, leaving his beloved hungry and thirsty like a starving beast. In this way it was revealed to them, unfortunately to both, that the love and passion that had once wrapped around them with overflowing abundance and devouring fire was now simply part of the past, before which Esmeralda decided to dedicate herself to his care and the recovery of his health, with a true longing to get back the loving man that she missed so much, her Sweetheart.

In that the doorbell rang, it was Johnny, with whom they would have lunch to celebrate Todd's birthday. He jumped off the bed and went down the stairs as he quickly dressed. Esmeralda looked out the window curious to meet Johnny, and in that she heard them argue, Johnny retracting the invitation to lunch knowing that Esmeralda would accompany them. Enraged, he grabbed his bicycle and took off, leaving his father gaping, shattered and furious.

Esmeralda was aware and felt truly guilty that, for Todd's children, it had been a tragedy that their father abandoned them when he began dating her, a situation that she had become aware of only in this reencounter, after twenty years. When they had met in Chile, he had introduced himself as a separated man and father of three children, but he wasn't separated, they lived under the same roof, although they hadn't been married for several years, the typical tale of unfaithful men. He wouldn't break the rule dragging Esmeralda to fall madly in love with him; if she had known he lived with his wife and children, she would have never allowed herself free rein to love.

Although the day of his birthday was quite traumatic, they had dinner at a beautiful restaurant; she managed to get the waitress to bring him a cake with a candle, she sang him happy birthday and they returned home to enjoy the surprise celebration. Between laughs, they ate and drank, and went to bed like two little elders, cuddling their naked bodies with infinite tenderness. The next morning, her cell phone had more than forty missed calls, all from Terry, who was a nutcase when he sensed his beloved Esmeralda's infidelity. It wasn't difficult for her to convince him that her battery had died, and when it was getting late and she was unable to return home, because she didn't manage to catch the last train before the station closed, she stayed with her sick friend. Cleverly and purposefully, she had posted on Facebook her location at St. Thomas' Hospital, with a photo taken walking down one of the hospital's clean and endless corridors. It was her perfect alibi to spend the night away from home and share the birthday celebration with her Sweetheart.

Esmeralda began to prepare her departure; the time had come to risk it all for her true love, so elusive in the past, and she wasn't going to let him get away under any circumstance, even loving Terry, although not with the madness and passion with which she loved Todd. As a well-dressed woman, her wardrobe was colossal, closets and drawers crammed with everything and more to perfectly combine dresses and pants with shoes, handbags, coats, jackets and scarves; She owned raincoats of all colors and styles, being her passion, it was very difficult for her to get rid of them, and kept most of them. She gave a lot of her stuff to charity, and this time it wasn't as painful to part with as it had been when she moved from Chile to England. She had learned to live with detachments and appreciate the meaning of things, memories, and experiences, above the material and superfluous, starting a new path in her life, that of minimalism.

Having made the firm decision to move in with Todd, she tried to find the best time to break the news to Terry. It was a tennis night, the day he returns home at 10:30 p.m. She thought of all the ways she could start the conversation…. and then she decided to wait for his arrival, while she prepared a sandwich and poured herself a couple of double whiskeys to have more courage and be able to face the difficult and delicate situation. At that moment, the sound of the keys opening the door surprised her with his arrival, an hour earlier than usual; he approached smiling to greet her with a kiss on the lips, to which she responded with a soft touch of her lips, asking:

–What happened? Why have you returned home so early?

He responds with sweetness and infinite love, looking into her eyes:

–I wanted to be with you, I miss you. We haven't made love in several nights …I need to feel you close… I need to feel that you're mine!!!

–Aaaaah… –she replies with a sigh, and listening to him. She couldn't feel guiltier being the villain of the movie, an unfaithful wife.

In that, he breaks the silence and adds with love:

–That's why, as soon as the tennis match ended, I came straight home without hanging out with my friends at the bar.

Esmeralda couldn't wait any longer, the wait was tormenting her. The anguish was making it difficult for her to breathe, accelerating her heartbeat. With a soft and firm tone, she dares to say the first words:

–I need to talk to you…

–He looked at her with an expression of curiosity and nervousness, finishing hanging up his sports jacket and putting away the bag in which he usually carries his tennis racket and other sports attire. He sits at the head of the table, and she gently takes him firmly by the hands, implying that the purpose of the

65

conversation was serious and important. Cautiously, trying to cause the least damage, a pain that is inevitable, she begins:

–Do you remember…how I mentioned that I am a free woman…even loving you and being married to you…

–Yes…I remember, and… –he responds in a tone of greater curiosity, wanting to know what she was trying to tell him.

–You reacted; you reminded me that I was married to you and therefore I wasn't free…you even showed me my wedding band…–he interrupts her again, even more intrigued:

–Yes…and?

She continues in a soft and slow tone…

–Well…on that occasion…we agreed that if one day…you or I…were interested in someone else…we would be honest and immediately let each other know…

–Yes, I remember very well. I said that! –raising his voice.

–It's just that…

–Ah, you're leaving me? –he asks in a loud and bothered tone.

–Yes, I'm leaving!!!

–You've met someone? Are you seeing someone else? Are you cheating on me? Tell me, don't lie to me.

–Yes, there's another person.

–Do I know him, have you slept with him? Tell me...tell me...don't lie!!!

–Please calm down....it doesn't make sense to ask so many questions...

–Are you trying to tell me that you're moving in with another man? Is that what you wanted to talk to me about?

–Yes, I'm leaving.

–We have to get divorced.

–Yes, of course. We don't have children together, so the divorce will be easier. I won't ask you for anything, only to get my freedom back.

–So, when do you plan on leaving?

–As soon as possible.

The atmosphere became tense and very sad, both about to cry, they naturally hugged each other, as if wanting to support each other and saying goodbye at the same time. Then he sat down holding his head with both hands, while tears dripped on the table cloth. His agitated breathing contained tears, anger, grief and frustration; the news had surprised him... he even thinks out loud:

—How stupid I've been, I hadn't realized it, and I wanting us to make love... —he shakes his head from side to side and Esmeralda rushes up to the second floor, takes refuge in the guest room, which becomes her new bedroom, and for the first time they sleep separately under one roof, as husband and wife. She tosses and turns in bed unable to fall asleep, feeling a deep sorrow for the one she still loves and yet abandoned for another great love.

The next day, she rushed to get her things ready, and even Terry suggested renting a Van, or better yet, asking a mutual friend for help who had an appropriate vehicle for moving furniture, and so she did. Within two days, Esmeralda had moved in with Todd. Todd's welcome was euphoric, he wanted her with him, and they quickly arranged Esmeralda's belongings, while others went to the attic, the same place where Maria's belongings had been hidden.

On one occasion, he told her, with a hint of frustration and regret, that since he was a child, he had dreamt of seeing Torres del Paine and the Chilean Patagonia. He remembered being almost in a trance when he saw a couple of photographs, dazzled by that wonderful expression of nature, so much so that he promised himself he would travel as soon as he could, a wish that had remained unfulfilled in the sphere of dreams. Despite having financial solvency, time and the great desire to visit that enchanted land, but not having someone to travel with, his dream was postponed. Esmeralda laughs out loud, boasting of her ability to travel alone wherever she wanted and wherever her magical red shoes would take her to live and enjoy a new adventure, omitting the innumerable occasions before the magic of her red shoes, in which she had had her suitcases packed without being able to travel when her companion desisted, usually a friend of those who says yes to everything but cancels at the last moment, or simply disappears from the face of the earth like Lieutenant Bello. Not to mention the time she went to Sharm el-Sheikh, an Arab land where, upon arrival at the airport, she felt the terror of not knowing how to communicate in Arabic or English, stunned by a all the prejudices and stories regarding Arab culture, where women still in XXI century have no right to anything, suffer all kinds of discrimination, and are forced to cover their faces with a veil, burqa and hijab. She was terrified, looking around for help, clinging on to two English couples, who, seeing her alone, frightened and defenseless, welcomed her with affection and admirable generosity, protecting her like a child, and as soon as she felt safe, she didn't take long in doing her own thing; she got along like a fish in water, without understanding or speaking a single word in Arabic and handling a squalid vocabulary of English.

They were fears and risks that her beloved Todd didn't share, being a calculating man. He seemed to admire and enjoy not only her beauty, joy and spontaneous personality, but also her serene and secure part, like a diva and goddess of Olympus, an image he fell for in the presence of her sparkling gaze and that of a successful woman. That was how they planed their trip to Chile, him trying to convince her of something that she didn't need convincing, because she dreamt as much or more than him to travel to her beloved Chile. She would finally be able to meet and snuggle Anthonella, her new granddaughter, who would be six months old, and he for his part but together with her, would make his dream come true of touring the immaculate and wonderful Chilean Patagonia and the Torres del Paine. In this way, they ventured to Chile for three months; Esmeralda jumped with joy, unable to believe that for the first time she would travel with her beloved Sweetheart and for a period of three months, bearing in mind that her trips never lasted more than two or three weeks. He, fuddled with drugs and depression therapies, along with rampant alcoholism from which he was imprisoned with no way out no matter how much therapy he received and no matter how many promises he made to himself, his children and Esmeralda, delegated all the responsibility to her in programming the trip in its entirety. She had to purchase the plane tickets, make the hotel reservations, tours, car rental, everything that was necessary, except the purchase of domestic flight tickets to the interior of Chile, which Esmeralda paid for with her own money and her own decision. He gave her one of his credit cards to pay the reservations and online purchases; Esmeralda wrote down every penny she spent and before doing so, informed him of all the purchase possibilities, offers and in particular, when the prices seemed high. He spared no expense, but would later reproach her for the large sum of money invested. The trip fulfilled the two main goals, although it wasn't exempt from vicissitudes; he slept very badly, suffered from nightmares and insomnia, even taking sleeping pills prescribed by the treating psychiatrist. He talked in his sleep, argued fiercely, cried, shouted and even threw slaps and kicks. Esmeralda hugged him giving him protection and comfort, calming him down for short periods of time. During the day he spent countless hour with his cell phone and tablet in hand, and when asked what he was doing, he would reply that he was reading the news from the United Kingdom and the United States. But in addition to being informed of what was happening worldwide, he talked to Elizabeth every day, his journalist friend. He was also very interested in knowing the ups and downs of the stock market, and although it's true that he read the news daily and leafed through the stock market, his real concern was to communicate with Maria, with whom he messaged on WhatsApp and sent endless emails to on a daily basis, always about the same thing, mutual reproaches of situations experienced, complaints and misunderstandings. It was undeniable that despite all the harm they had done to each other in the recent past, the wounds never stopped bleeding, there were indestructible ties between them that kept them united by fire, such as her father's terminal illness and the fact that he had died in Todd's arms. There was also the engagement, why would he marry her? It could be said that, to please Maria's father, who suffered seeing his youngest daughter so alone, unlucky in love, a single mother, and living with someone other than the father of her daughter; he couldn't die leaving his daughter helpless, it was the greatest pain that afflicted him, more than the cancer that consumed his life day by day. When they made him part of the great news that Maria was finally getting married, he clung to Todd, loving him as one of his own children.

The dental clinic project would expand and be transformed into a beauty and health clinic, as a strategy to captivate Renata's interest. She was initially stunned by the results she could have on her patients' faces, restoring youth, beauty and raising their self-esteem, security and confidence. She could be a true facial architect, in addition to the fact that it was a very lucrative business with an exquisite public.

When the social outbreak known as the *Estadillo Social* occurred in Chile, the country became insecure and unstable to live a normal daily life; a social movement that began with the burning of buses and subway/metro stations, as a reaction to the $30 rise in ticket prices. There were daily demontrations, street closures, suspension of public transportation, burning of cars and commercial premises, intervention in the expeditious and free traffic of both pedestrians and vehicles, with the consequent action of the police, which used tear gas, water and rubber bullets against the protestors, generating an atmosphere of insecurity, hysteria and collective fear. Businesses began to close early or as soon as they heard that a group of protesters were approaching, seriously damaging the normal development of the country in all aspects. Educational establishments suspended classes, there were even days when it was authorized not to go to work or it was simply not possible to get to them due to the impossibility of traveling by public or private transportation. All of this had a negative impact on the development of commerce and, obviously, of the clinic; For the same reason patients began to arrive late or simply couldn't assist, canceling their appointments; doctors couldn't arrive either, and when they did, they worked only during the morning shift and if it was possible until the middle of the afternoon, and even on some occasions, at noon they were forced to close and run to reach any means of transport back to their homes. In the days of severe riots, transportation stopped working for safety reasons and because the same protesters impeded normal traffic, closing off streets, knocking down traffic lights and setting buses and even cars on fire, becoming something habitual for students and workers to walk hours and hours to return home. On the other hand, when economic income decreased due to the lack of patients and the impossibility of working normally, a debt was generated due to the payment of fixed expenses, such as basic services and rent, in addition to the payment of salaries. She was confident that the protests would end soon, which in general and traditionally didn't last more than two or three days, and in other cases, occasionally, for a few months and only for half the day, with demonstrations in front of the main government buildings. In other instances, before which multitudes of people crowded around demanding improvements in social and environmental welfare, Esmeralda, and probably the entire country, never thought that the social outbreak could last for months and exceed a couple of years.

From the first moment that Todd and Esmeralda set foot on Chilean soil, upon their arrival at the Arturo Merino Benítez airport in Santiago de Chile, they were faced with the first glimpses of the political and social crisis in which the country was submerged. Esmeralda was impressed by how the streets of Santiago looked and the tormented faces of passers-by, perceiving a mixture of nervousness and stress in the people with whom they interacted. Graffiti, scribbling on buildings, and streets plagued with slogans against the government. The political class and social demands were the new clothing of the Chilean capital, images that were displayed throughout the country with a notable concentration in the regional capitals and main cities of the country. The smell of smoke from the fires and barricades, added to the acidic air from the tear gas canisters, were another sign of the social outbreak, affecting their tear ducts, throat and nose. Shop windows, walls and doors of commercial premises fortified with steel sheets, as safety measures to prevent entry and looting, dismantling and fires, were palpable and evident images of chaos, violence and insecurity, generating despair, suffering, pain and increasing poverty levels of the Chilean population; a desolated panorama that increased as they moved away from the airport towards the hotel, giving Esmeralda the impression that it wasn't her beloved Chile, while Todd looked horrified and incredulous at what the beauty and prosperity of the leading country of South America had become. It was a big impact seeing Plaza Baquedano completely destroyed, devoid of the slightest memory of the colorful and fragrant gardens, and the imposing statue of General Baquedano with his steed remained upright, although covered in graffiti and painted in blood. The convulsed scenario of the streets of Santiago, although true, were repeated in the main cities and regional capitals, thankfully in less quantity and level of destruction, evidenced in the journey through much of the extreme south, center and small north, initiated with a veil in the city of Aysén to fulfill Todd's long-awaited trip to the Chilean Patagonia.

So yes, Esmeralda and Todd traveled to Chile, despite everything, and strategically opted to stay at a hotel in the Lastarria neighborhood, a bohemian neighborhood in the center of the city, considered by locals and outsiders as the coolest in Santiago in terms of tourism.

She wanted to show her Sweetheart the most beautiful and interesting places in her country, and she thought that Lastarria would be the most appropriate due to its historical and cultural richness, since writers, painters, musicians and architects had lived there and everything breathed of attractive intellectual and artistic air. They were close to the Museum of Contemporary Art, the National Museum of Fine Arts —she told him proudly that it was the oldest in Latin America—, the Museum of Visual Arts and the Gabriela Mistral Center.

Everything was perfect, except for the fact that they were close to the demonstrations. Although the social outbreak had occurred in October, in the following months the tension had continued to grow. In fact, the riots continued until March of the following year, 2020. Esmeralda, out of interest in her country and her own profession, followed with great interest all the events that occurred before her eyes, and her heart broke with sadness and fear of the unleashed violence she saw on the streets.

Not only the demonstrations themselves, but also the destruction, looting, fires and hatred that people seemed to have in their souls, evidenced the extreme division of the Chilean society.

It all started or was sparked by the announcement of the increase in the Santiago Metro fare, which caused literally thousands of high school students to organize themselves to carry out acts of mass evasion in the Metro. These acts consisted of jumping and avoiding the payment mechanisms of public transportation, and as the days passed, more people joined this form of protest.

The increase in fare was the trigger to unleash great social dissatisfaction, hidden for decades under the premise that Chile was the most advanced and developed country in Latin America, perhaps, but it was also one of the most unequal, from a social and economic point of view.

They considered that the increase was inappropriate and unacceptable in the midst of the economic crisis, with low wages, high rates of unemployment and an inefficient and unsatisfactory train service. There were also delays in the schedules and there weren't enough trains, which caused agglomerations of passengers, who, aggressively and desperately, tried to get on the railroad cars in order to get to work or their studies on time; in short, to fulfill their responsibilities or reach their destinations. It was a situation that was repeated at the beginning and at the end of each day; all this caused the thefts to multiply, not to mention that women passengers suffered abuse from some criminals who took advantage and touched them, pretending that it was accidental due to the movement of the train and how crowded they were. On October 25, 2019, there was a great mobilization that brought together 1.2 million people in the streets demanding social justice; that would be a historic day, the largest march since the return of democracy to the country. It was a massive march that took over the streets of the center of the Chilean capital, protesting social inequality in the country and demanding the implementation of profound social reforms. According to government figures quoted by local media, indeed, more than 1.2 million people gathered in Plaza Italia and surrounding streets, a nerve center of the Chilean capital. Citizens of different origins, of all social classes, ideologies and creeds, families with children, people with disabilities, the elderly and even patients in wheelchairs joined the clamor of the Chilean people, who gathered united in a single cry for social justice and equity. The crowds that walked through the streets of Santiago to attend the march brought traffic to a standstill in the Chilean capital. The march took place in a festive atmosphere totally different from the climate of anxiety of the first days of the crisis outbreak. To the cries of "Chile woke up" and "The people united will never be defeated", thick columns of protesters advanced through the central avenue in Santiago. Although the march was mostly peaceful, groups of hooded men caused some disturbances and the police used water and tear gas to disperse the protesters. After hours of peaceful marching, there were some incidents between demonstrators and the police... In addition to the most repeated slogans: "Chile woke up" and "We are not at war", referring to the statement made by President Piñera against those who caused the fires at the metro stations and in supermarkets. Countless banners with different messages were seen among the protesters, such as: "Corrupt to jail" or "For the dignity of our people, to the streets without fear"; "I don't march for Chile, I pray for a better Chile"; "For a dignified country"; "I hope that Chile is a more dignified country to live in"; "A dignified country"; "Deserving pensions, not the PFAs" –Pension Fund Administrators–, the latter being precisely one of the demands of the Chilean population, the modification of the pension system and improvement of the health service with the establishment of a universal and free health and education system. Among the banners and cheers from protesters, people were also heard shouting and calling for the resignation of President Piñera.

One of the most emotionally charged moments during the march, was probably when thousands of people sang *El baile de los que sobran* "The dance of those left over" the iconic song by the group Los Prisioneros, which became popular in the 1980s as a protest and criticism of social inequality and the lack of opportunities in Chile. Others protested playing the song by Víctor Jara *El derecho de vivir en paz* "The right to live in peace." During the social outbreak there were real pitched battles between the protesters and the *carabineros* or police Special Forces, and even being in the Chilean capital, Esmeralda and Todd saw each other involved in two demonstrations as passers-by and eager to feel in situ the reality that was lived in Chile. They had to run through the streets fleeing the violence and the police, unable to breathe because of the tear gas acid.

Going out to restaurants was complicated, the bar and café owners warned them of the dangers of staying outside, on the terrace, but they preferred to take the risk of having protesters pass by and take whatever they were eating or drinking, wanting to see firsthand and be part, to a certain extent, of the clamor of the people fighting for everyone's well-being.

Plaza Baquedano, also known as Plaza Italia, and later with the social outbreak, known as Plaza Dignidad, was the meeting point for protesters and the place where the marches were convened. The sectors surrounding this square, such as the Lastarria neighborhood –where Esmeralda and Todd's hotel was located – were the scene of unbridled vandalism; The centenary temple of San Francisco de Borja, as well as the church of La Asunción, were reduced to ashes.

On the other hand, other residential and very old sectors of Santiago with construction buildings of more than a hundred years, where huge mansions stood tall, the vast majority in poor state of conservation and uninhabited, giving the impression that they were abandoned, began to be inhabited by squatters, a term that identifies those who, without being owners, occupy a house to live, generally young Chileans, artists, anarchists, enemies of the prevailing system and the traditions of the conventional family, followed by criminals, and in the last years by migrants from neighboring countries. Artists, who were part of the social outbreak, transformed immense walls into true works of art, paintings that reflected their struggle, their origin, their unsatisfied demands, complaints and satires to the authorities of the moment and to the political class in general, highlighting their leaders and heroes. The presence of Chavismo and Che Guevara drew attention, as well as artists who have been icons and victims of social struggles by losing their lives, assassinated by government repression, amongst them the international referent of the protest song, the singer-songwriter Victor Jara, arrested after September 11, 1973, the date of the coup by the Chilean armed forces led by Army General Augusto Pinochet against President Salvador Allende. Victor Jara posed a threat to a military regime that sought to clip the wings of artists and silence citizens, and for this reason was arrested along with other teachers and students and transferred to the Chilean Stadium, which would later bear his name. Esmeralda translated for Todd a piece of news from that time: "What occurred from the day of his arrest until his death, on September 16, 1973, has yet to be clarified. However, with the passage of time, more and more testimonies appear within the shadows of the past. The first accused for the murder of Victor Jara, Commander César Manríquez Bravo, was the head of the improvised prison camp that was installed in the Chilean Stadium –a sports facility that since 2003 would bear the name of Victor Jara in his honor–. According to the soldier's own statement, inside the sports facility was a "Dante Alighieri-like scenery" due to the large number of prisoners –about 5,600–, as reported by the Journalistic Investigation Center (CIPER). That is how the military placed two machine guns on the building's balconies, which they called "Hitler's saws, capable of splitting a person in two". On the second floor, very powerful light bulbs were installed that remained on 24 hours a day, so that the detainees would lose track of time. According to what was reported, the first four days, both the prisoners and the military, were kept in unsanitary living conditions, without food and with sewage problems. According to Captain David Gonzalez Toro, in charge of supplies, it wouldn't be until September 16th that they would receive some rations for the soldiers. On the last day for Victor Jara, the same day that food arrived at the stadium, he lost his life. Around 6 p.m., a squad of soldiers arrived at the sports facility, where they were ordered to monitor the compound's transmission booths. Several testimonies affirm that Victor Jara was detained at the place together with the director of the band Los Prisioneros, Liter Quiroga, and the director of investigations Eduardo Coco Paredes. Hours later, Lieutenant Pedro Barrientos arrived at the room where two soldiers were guarding the singer-songwriter. At that moment, those present began to insult him for his condition as a communist. Later, as the main witness recalls, one of the soldiers, who was guarding him, sent him back to his cabin. As night fell, the witness commented that the soldier took some 15 detainees into the subway, including Victor Jara. One of the soldiers began to play Russian roulette with his revolver, resting it on the singer-songwriter's temple. With that diabolical pastime, Victor Jara received a mortal shot on his temple. According to the witness, he saw how his body fell to the ground, on its side and convulsing, before which soldiers began to shoot at him relentlessly, receiving 44 bullet wounds in his body, as the autopsy later indicated. That is how the military put an end to the four days of torture and suffering of the singer-songwriter, during which he had been subjected to at least two interrogations in the compound rooms, where he had been the subject of numerous tortures, including his hands being fractured after several blows from a pistol grip, according to CIPER. The last prisoners who saw Victor Jara alive say that his body was full of bruises and his face was swollen. His remains, which would spend days at the entrance of the sports facility along with other corpses, were found by officials from the

First Police Station of Renca, who transferred him to the legal medicine institute without knowing his identity. Almost 43 years after the incident, in June 2016, a federal court in the United States found former military officer Barrientos guilty of extrajudicially torturing and executing the singer-songwriter, activist and politician. Barrientos, born in Chile, who would later become a US citizen with residence in the state of Florida, was found guilty after the accusation was filed by the singer-songwriter's widow and his two daughters, demanding a 28 million dollar compensation from the ex-lieutenant, according to the newspaper La Tercera"...

Todd, saddened by feelings of rage and impotence in the face of such reprehensible acts, made an effort to raise his voice and thank Esmeralda for informing him of the events that occurred after the coup in Chile. Likewise, she made it easier for him to understand and interpret the artists' paintings... The artists of the social outbreak, who, through their works, made known the origin, causes and objectives of their mobilization; in their paintings, the images of the reprisals who suffered because of the police and soldiers who took to the streets occupy a relevant role. Another symbol reflected in the paintings is the presence of the "Negro Matapacos" –an icon dog of social resistance in Chile–. Negro Matapacos was a Chilean dog that gained notoriety due to its presence in the street protests that took place in Santiago de Chile during 2010; among its characteristics was its black fur and the red scarf it wore tied around its neck, although he also wore a blue colored scarf and a white one, which were placed by the students. The dog, originally named by its owner simply as "El Negro", gained notoriety among university circles in Santiago, mainly at the University of Santiago (USACH), Metropolitan University of Technology (UTEM) and Central University of Chile (UCEN). During the 2011 protests, Negro Matapacos earned his nickname and became known for appearing during street marches barking at and threatening the *pacos* – an idiom used in Chile to refer to the carabineros, the police Special Forces– which generated sympathy among the protesters. It would continue with its appearances in demonstrations throughout the decade, gaining fame among students and citizens who took pictures of the dog and shared them on social media, even creating a profile dedicated to Negro Matapacos on Facebook. Although the dog was considered a stray, due to its presence in different university campuses and streets of Santiago, Negro Matapacos was under the care of Maria Campos, a resident of Garcia Reyes Street in the Santiago commune, located a few blocks from the USACH on the avenue, who adopted him in 2009 and who fed him; She had a bed for him in her residence. She tied the scarves he used around his neck and also blessed him before he went out. According to his participation in street protests, several media networks also called him the Chilean *Loukanikos*, due to his similarities with the dog that became famous during the protests in Greece between 2010 and 2012. There were at least two incidents in which he was injured: a fight with another dog at the UTEM, and another time he was run over by a police car, being treated at the Alberto Hurtado University. Negro Matapacos passed away on August 26, 2017 due to natural causes, attended by veterinary staff and his caregivers. Various sources mention that at the time of his death he had left an offspring of thirty-two puppies with six different female dogs. During the 2019 protests, the image of Negro Matapacos once again gained notoriety due to his attitude during the street demonstrations, appearing on various posters, stickers, murals, paper-mache sculptures, comics, video games and three-dimensional reproductions, and even requesting to install a statue of the dog in Plaza Baquedano. Tributes to the dog have also appeared in other Chilean cities, such as a statue in Iquique and a mural in Temuco, as well as an altar with a statue of the dog outside the Gabriela Mistral Cultural Center in Santiago.

A shocking and very painful aspect that generated repudiation at a national and international level, were the attacks against the protesters with projectiles and rubber bullets, some of whom came to have partial and total loss of sight, as well as the loss of one of their eyes, and some even lost both eyes.

Among the protesters who partially or totally lost their sight as a result of the impact of rubber bullets, is Fabiola Andrea Campillai Rojas, Chilean activist and politician, who became known nationally and internationally by losing her sight due to a shot fired by a police officer, an event that occurred during the social outbreak in October 2019. On the night of November 26, 2019, during the social outbreak, she left her house in San Bernardo to go work the night shift at a Carozzi factory. A group of police officers were watching some rioters, although other sources mention that there weren't any at that time. When she was waiting at a bus stop, a policeman located fifty meters away, threw a tear gas canister that hit her in the face. Upon impact, she fell to the ground and lost consciousness. Police Forces continued to fire tear gas and then left without providing medical assistance, despite the fact that at least two police officers saw that a person had been injured. She was taken to a hospital by neighbors. As a result of the impact, her two eyeballs burst, she suffered a head injury, skull and face fractures, and was left blind, with no sense of smell and taste. She was in an induced coma and during the two months after the attack, underwent surgery three times. The National Institute of Human Rights (NIHR) filed a complaint against the police. The investigation lasted more than eight months and identified Patricio Maturana as responsible for launching the tear gas canister. He was expelled from the institution, accused of "unlawful coercion resulting in very serious injuries". The Prosecutor's Office carried out a second investigation, which revealed that Patricio Maturana wasn't certified to use a gas-launching shotgun on the date of the attack. The Prosecutor's Office requested twelve years in prison for the former officer. In the 2021 parliamentary elections, Fabiola

Campillai was elected, with the highest number of votes at the national level, as Senator of the Republic of Chile, as an independent, and representing District No. 7 of the Santiago Metropolitan Region, for the legislative period 2022-2026. She is one of the leaders who embraces the enactment of a presidential pardon law for all people detained as a result of the riots of the social outbreak, mostly young people and even minors, who upon being detained and after verifying their identity and age, their freedom is determined by the Law of Criminal Responsibility for Adolescents. This law determines three types of sanctions: deprivation of liberty, non-deprivation of liberty and accessory sanctions. The deprivation of liberty sanctions are internment in a closed and semi-closed regime, in addition to accessory sanctions. Consequently, adolescents over 14 and under 18 today can be charged, tried and sentenced by the courts, although under a special statute that is much less punitive than the common law applicable to adults. For adolescents between 14 and 15 years of age, the maximum sentence of imprisonment is eight years.

The symbol that represents the loss of an eye, and in extreme cases, the loss of both, due to the impact of rubber bullets with the consequent explosion of the eyeball, is widespread throughout the country, painting bloody eyes, represented in a red blood-color, rolling to the ground. Many images of faces are found on the streets, statues, sculptures, monuments and buildings, everywhere, and not only faces, but also pools and waterfalls are painted with blood, shocking scenes that shake even the most incredulous of what happened. Today, thanks to social media it is possible to know everything that happens in the world and immediately, even through live transmissions, becoming true sources of information, entertainment, knowledge and denunciation. Well, it was made public how infiltrators caused destruction, graffiti and fires; civilians wearing police uniforms posing as them to set fires and vice versa, or people with one eye covered with an eye patch pretending to be victims of the police and appearing at marches, posing for photojournalists and giving false statements to national and international mass media.

Esmeralda, being part of the mobilizations as a spectator, on her way through Santiago de Chile and staying in a hotel in the Lastarria neighborhood, just one block from the Alameda, was able to hear, feel and suffer the effects of the tear gas canisters, particularly on Friday nights, with the effervescence of the demontraions, which acquired a terrible climate of violence, and the disturbances becoming unbelievable. The reckless and irreverent behavior of the hooded men shook every window, lighthouse, public lights and traffic lights. Prudence indicated it was time to leave the conflict zone as soon as it began to get dark or things began to get heated, which generally arose with the arrival and attitude of the police, throwing water with the *"Huanaco"* –a car that throws water from the Special Forces to break up riots–, trying to dissuade the protesters, who responded by throwing stones and firebombs, among other projectiles, generating a true pitched battle. The levels of aggression on both sides had risen, the tear gas canisters and the blast of the pellets turned out to be highly effective, the demonstrators, and even more so the bystanders and onlookers, walked terrified in search of a safety zone, while some of the protestors were taken and detained by the police and placed in detention vehicles, before the astonished gaze of their comrades in struggle, who unsuccessfully try to avoid arrests.

The demonstrations and marches of the social outbreak, which took place practically daily and religiously every Friday, were peaceful marches, but inevitably, as the end of each mobilization approached, the atmosphere began to tense; the tension could be sensed as it turned into vandalism and crime, utter chaos and devastation, destruction of everything in their path and more.

The Special Forces and the Chilean police unsuccessfully tried to break up the demonstrations, appease and reduce the protestors to regain normality. A series of fires and destruction of emblematic and historical places set the tone for the riots; Likewise, other properties of great historical, cultural and traditional connotation of the Chilean population considered by the protesters didn't escape the clutches of hatred and the destruction of the hooded people: representative monuments of capitalism, and others built as symbols of colonization and domination of the Chilean people by the hands of the conquerors, invaders and assassins. Acts of vandalism occurred throughout the country, concentrating in the regional capitals. With a look of flabbergast and horror, viewers watched the live broadcast of the uncontrollable burnings of churches, temples and chapels from the Colonial period, various monuments and government and educational establishments, even universities, looting of supermarkets and shopping centers, improvised barricades with furniture stolen from robbed and destroyed establishments, such as banks, educational centers, pension administrators' offices and private health centers. In short, everything was piled up in the middle of the streets forming gigantic incendiary barricades, causing chaos and interrupting vehicular and even pedestrian traffic. The fires in the Santiago Metro were made in response to the rise in ticket prices; churches were burnt down in rejection and repudiation of the abuse of minors by priests, as well as shopping malls and banks in rejection of neoliberalism and capitalism.

Esmeralda and her Sweetheart began their journey to the south of Chile. Her frenzy and joy at being in Punta Arenas would be nothing compared to the ecstasy of reaching the foot of the wonderful and famous Torres del Paine, reaching its summit with her heart and soul. The thickness and luxuriance of the forests, lakes and mountains, the diversity of floral species, wildlife and animals kept him ecstatic; he hugged Esmeralda with enormous strength, in a gesture of joy and gratitude for having made his dream come true, the one he had treasured since he was a child: traveling to Chile and seeing the Patagonia. The days became like nothingness itself, like a sigh, promising to return as soon as possible and staying longer to delight in the native and virginal landscapes of a true earthly paradise. The local gastronomy was exquisite and the candlelight dinners united them and strengthened their love as a couple. Every day, Todd experienced improvements in his general state of health, reflected in his physical appearance, the sparkle in his eyes, greater energy, joy and vitality, along with all that, his virility, a fact that made him very happy, sticking out his chest like a peacock with the moans of pleasure that he extorted from his beloved Esmeralda.

Like a couple of newlyweds, they walked hand in hand and embraced the Chilean south; in Puerto Montt they were received by a married couple, friends of Esmeralda and with whom they toured the island of Angelmó by boat, Frutillar, Lake Todos los Santos, with its waterfalls and currents of fresh turquoise waters, among other wonderful touristic places in southern Chile. They stayed at their friend's house in Valdivia; after an exquisite barbecue, empanadas and table talk, to the beat of music and the guitar, for the first time in their lives they joined in on the fun and danced, becoming a moment of total euphoria for Esmeralda, who didn't stop shouting to her friends and to the four winds in the parcel:

—Look, we're dancing for the first time, yes, for the first time. I'm so, so happy, I can't believe it! —she hugged and kissed him again and again; he seemed happier than usual and offered to pick up the plates and leftovers from the barbecue to take from the patio to the kitchen. She wanted to help, but the owner of the house prevents her:

—Let him do it, he's happy. Let him feel useful. Let him enjoy feeling like he's at home.

That day he drank more than usual; he became tired and fell asleep at sundown without being able to enjoy the wonderful sunset reflected in the Calle-Calle River; irrelevant facts in the face of the happiness that overwhelmed them. From Valdivia they traveled to Pucón, a favorite vacationing area in Chile, since her children were little. Esmeralda and her family used to enjoy the summer vacation season, unforgettable for everyone; the children jumped for joy when it rained in the middle of summer, unlike any tourist who would feel bad not being able to enjoy a day at the beach, swimming in the lake or practicing some mountain sport or sailing in the river. Rain and cold were synonymous with hot springs, there being no greater pleasure than bathing in the warm hot springs under the rain; they loved the steam that was generated by the contrast in temperatures, assimilating the image with the typical London fog. They enjoyed the soft tingling feeling under their feet when walking on the warm pebbles that were on the bottom of the pools, going down to the river next to the thermal pools, and jumping over the suspension bridge to cause a greater swing. Those were family vacations just as or more wonderful than the ones experienced at Disney World.

Being in the south of Chile, she wasn't going to miss the chance of sharing such a wonderful experience with her beloved Todd, the happiness that invaded them highlighted Esmeralda's humorous and mischievous facet; she made jokes alluding to the fact that she feared that her Sweetheart would melt with the high summer temperatures and the thermal waters. He replied laughing with a mischievous face:

—Don't worry, my darling, beers and fine Chilean wine will keep me intact for you, so you can devour me, you glutton, haha!

Effectively, they enjoyed a relaxing day in the hot springs, they even took a dip in the cold waters of one of the Trancura River streams; they crossed the suspension bridge, but not before stopping and posing for posterity, kissing one more time and telling each other how happy they were. Back north, they met at the Santiago airport with Esmeralda's mother, whom they had

94

invited to vacation with them for a week in the beautiful resort of Bahía Inglesa; This was an opportunity that would allow her to spend time with her great-grandchildren and allow Esmeralda to see Victoria and her adorable little grandchildren, calming her impatience to meet Anthonella, her new granddaughter. Since arriving at the beach, Victoria had avoided seeing her mother and kept the children away from their grandmother, but not from their great-grandmother. Todd became frustrated and angry when he saw Esmeralda crying inconsolably at the impossibility of being with her grandchildren; she had planned to see them, play with them, give them their gifts and hug her new granddaughter close to her chest.

She couldn't understand that; knowing Esmeralda's sweetness, tenderness and boundless love for her grandchildren and her children, although the relationship with them had become distant after the divorce. Victoria once again shattered her mother's heart; an expert in manipulation, she denied her, as usual, the right to see and spend time with her grandchildren, Esmeralda's Achilles heals. It broke her heart, transforming her into an endless stream of tears, and as always, Victoria planned her father's visit to the beach during the time in which Esmeralda was in Chile, the perfect excuse to prevent her from seeing the children, due to the incompatibility of her parents' personalities. Her father had the privilege of spending time with his daughter and grandchildren, since he financially supported Victoria and her family, generosity as immeasurable as the reciprocal manipulation between them, of a strange but real love between father and daughter. Victoria was an expert in changing situations and using them at her convenience, playing the role of victim, making her mother the villain, an inhumane and selfish person, and cataloging her as the world's worst mother, completely forgetting and not recognizing at all, and perhaps unaware of it, that she spent her childhood with an absent father, as he was immersed in work, which in turn was the perfect excuse to unleash his inexhaustible chain of infidelities. They had been children raised in the care of nannies and under the supervision of a mother who was wounded, irritable, hysterical and devastated by the extreme domestic violence and marital crisis, a harsh reality and suffering that her children were largely unaware of, thanks to the fact that Esmeralda tried to keep them on the sidelines to avoid further psychological and personal damage; and on the other hand, as adolescents, they lived in their own bubble, and when they saw their parents arguing they isolated themselves, locked in their rooms, with the music turned up, or simply with headphones, while Esmeralda was being attacked without mercy by the person who swore her eternal love, protection and respect. Mario became something else, transforming into a monster that spewed out lava as he unleashed a rosary of insults and slanders against his wife; From his reddened eyes, product of demonic anger, real flames of fire sprouted, from the inquisitive way in

96

which he looked at poor Esmeralda, who responded furiously, using a remarkably more prudent vocabulary, insulting him only when referring to the infidelities.

To cut a long story short, the day before returning to London, and after having managed to hold a couple of fleeting encounters with her grandchildren, but not before receiving insults and even death threats from Victoria, who was unsettled just by hearing her mother's name and even more knowing that she was close by, Esmeralda found out, through her mother, that Victoria was getting married in the next few days. She was finally formalizing her relationship with the father of her children, after living together for more than ten years. It would be a private event without involving Vittorio's family, who from the beginning of the relationship were drastically against her and not to mention a marriage, even and despite the fact that they loved each other and were expecting a child. Meanwhile they were inviting Victoria's father, who had obviously also purchased their wedding bands.

A strong incident shook Esmeralda's life during her stay in Bahía Inglesa: the sudden death of her young and dear friend Juan Manuel, who was a couple of years younger than her. He died on a Sunday. After having breakfast with his wife, he went to the bedroom, sat on the edge of the bed and collapsed, dying almost instantly of a heart attack. In vain were the attempts to resuscitate him. Beatriz, his wife, and their son, quickly began cardiopulmonary resuscitation techniques; the paramedics who arrived soon after were unable to bring him back to life, despite intensifying chest compressions and mouth-to-mouth resuscitation, even using the defibrillation device.

She remembers that her friend, after undergoing a gastric sleeve and a stomach bypass to lose weight, was never the same again. He looked emaciated and his health deteriorated, worsening completely when he fell from his horse; He broke his clavicle, an arm and three ribs, one of them puncturing his lung. He remained hospitalized for months with vital risk before recovering much of his health. But even so, he returned to being a chain smoker, a habit that had been strictly prohibited; only for a few months did he respect the instructions of his doctor and family.

For Esmeralda it was a very strong blow; she cried like a baby when she received the news. During the funeral she supported her friend Beatriz, sharing the pain with countless friends and acquaintances that had come by the hundreds to share with the bereaved and say a last goodbye to their childhood friend, from his college years, mining work, barbecues, parties and good life. The return to Bahía Inglesa was contemplative, serene and of reflection; her strength was weakening and she was no longer willing to fight for her great love. That morning, before traveling to Copiapó, she had a serious talk with Todd, asking him to make up his mind once and for all, to stop living between two worlds, that his health was deteriorating, that living together wasn't healthy for him or her; it's impossible to have a relationship between three people, but he insisted that everything was over with Maria. However, he communicated with her daily and in his and in hours of sleeplessness he named her over and over again, with rage and pain. Esmeralda begged him to think and make a decision: he could go back to Maria, stay alone, or give himself entirely to the relationship with her.

During the stay in Bahía Inglesa, Esmeralda made Todd participate in her traditional yacht ride with her friend Leonardo and his wife. They sailed from the yacht club in the port of Caldera, located in front of the monument built in honor of the French researcher and marine biologist Jacques Cousteau, and in gratitude for his expeditions on the Chilean coast, including his passage through the port of Caldera. The day was ideal for sailing, temperatures bordering 24 degrees and with optimal winds to raise sails; everyone was part of the crew fulfilling different roles, from providing provisions, untying and unfurling sails, lifting anchors and releasing ropes from the dock. With the wind in favor, they set sail, popping champagne and toasting with Scotch whiskey. Seafood empanadas were the perfect lunch on the high seas. They talked about the human and the divine, while they took turns playing the role of captain, each steering with unequal skill and audacity, although the only true captain was obviously Leo.

Politics, the social outbreak and the Coronavirus became the main topic of conversation. Todd hardly participated in the conversations, he spent most of the time sitting in the bow with his eyes lost in the horizon, except when he agreed to take the helm and fish, retrieving the line and pulling out the prey, a Sea bass of almost eight kilograms, which would become the weekend feast for Leonardo's family, changing his role of captain for that of chef. Jaime, Esmeralda's younger and beloved brother, visited them frequently at the beach cabin where they stayed, even more so when he got to see his mother whom he didn't see as often as he would've liked, since he lived at the other end of the long and narrow Chile. With them they shared succulent barbecues until late at night between jokes, pranks and the open bar of mostly beer and whiskey; it couldn't be any other way.

Todd was very well received and integrated into the family, he seemed very cheerful and tried to converse as much as possible with his almost zero command of Spanish; it was very funny to see how he managed to make himself understood, although Esmeralda helped by translating. Todd's great regret, being a topic of conversation with Esmeralda's family, was Victoria's rejection of her mother and the great and unfair damage it caused her. He stated, in a strong and determined voice, that as soon as he had the opportunity to see her, he would have a serious conversation with her regarding her bad behavior and the great sorrow it caused her mother.

But this was left in pure intentions, since Victoria refused to meet Todd, and the couple of times she spent with Esmeralda and the children, the condition was that he couldn't be part of the activity, cataloging it as a family matter to which lovers weren't welcomed. Esmeralda could have mentioned that the exception didn't apply to her father's lovers; however, she preferred to remain silent and avoid comments in order to see her grandchildren and also her daughter, with whom she longed for an affective and close mother and daughter relationship.

Back in London, during the layover at Guarulhos International Airport in São Paulo, Brazil, immersed in the task of reading and responding to hundreds of unopened messages and emails received in the almost three months in Chile, Todd abruptly interrupted her, blurting out of the blue what he had probably planned for several days:

—Well…we have failed as a couple, like many others!!!

Esmeralda took a deep breath, making an effort to control the emotion of shock, looked at his face and with dignity and admirable serenity answered:

–Indeed, it's true, we're not doing well as a couple; we are very different.

–Yes, we are totally different; if you had spoken English when we first met, I would have never established a relationship with you, I would have distanced myself from you immediately –he replied with a tone of despisal and coldness.

–I would have also distanced myself from you; I would've been gone like the wind!!!

And she added with a vindictive sarcasm:

–Yes, we are extremely different, and you're also not a free person...

–I am free, I'm single!!! –He adds–: I've never been married; I didn't even marry the mother of my children. I don't understand what you're talking about. Why are you saying that I'm not a free person? –he insisted frowning and prying.

–And what about Maria?

–She doesn't exist!!! –he replies furiously raising his voice.

–Noooo, noooo, that's not true, you're lying, you talk to her every day. Or am I wrong? Are you going to deny it?

–No, we don't talk every day, only occasionally, and it's only because some of her things are still in my house, which I threw away because you told me to get rid of them —he lowers his voice and adds with a tone of regret —: I shouldn't have done it. Anyway, that's why we still communicate, nothing more; I don't care for her at all, she left and left my life.

At that moment, he reacted realizing that she knew more than she should, and rebuked her in an intimidating way:

—Have you been going through my WhatsApp messages?

She continued the conversation avoiding the answer, while he gave her an ultimatum:

—Yes, indeed we have failed as a couple, like many others. We have nothing in common, we are very different, and it doesn't make sense to continue trying; this relationship is impossible, it's gone out the window.

Esmeralda received the message reflexively, taking a few minutes to respond, because there was a lot at stake and not just the dream of a life together united by overflowing love and the enormous passion that had united them in the distant past. It was evident that twenty years hadn't passed in vain, but she wasn't going to give up, she still loved him despite seeing him so deteriorated, devoid of professional armor; today it was just him, without positions or professional titles, without the masks of foundations or international companies that dressed him with prestige and arrogance. Esmeralda was very aware of his alcohol addiction and how that had consumed his life, imprisoned in a severe depression, suffering from delusional hallucinations, an almost non-existent relationship with his children and an uncontrollable hatred towards their mother; in addition to the stormy relationship that he maintained with Maria, even despite the breakup, a breakup that he couldn't get over due to the unexpected, despite the fact that they argued daily, and the threats of abandonment and ending the relationship were constant. It was like the story of the boy who cried wolf, when it happened, nobody believed it and the blow was deadly. Her departure had annihilated him, it was evident that he was surprised, he was wasn't prepared to live once again the pain of contempt and the humiliation of being abandoned by a woman, an issue that is usually deadly in the life of a man, who supposedly is raised to be the leader of the pack, the virile macho, who is respected and loved above all else and under all circumstances. The fact that a woman abandons them annihilates them; abandonment leaves no man standing when feeling the relentless whiplash of despisal.

This situation reminded her of Mario, the father of her children, who went crazy after being abandoned by the woman of his life, the one he met in the fullness and beauty of his youth, vibrant, cheerful, naive and innocent, who had loved him with all her heart and soul, who forgave again and again his disloyalty, infidelity and aggression, who he was completely sure would never abandon him. However, it happened, completely annihilating his life, destroying and uprooting his virile image as an untouchable macho. He couldn't understand how she had left him, being at the peak of his professional career, providing her with all the luxury she wanted and more, without realizing it and even less recognizing that, thanks to his bad behavior as a macho and narcissistic man, his wife was being consumed in the abyss of sadness and depression, losing her sparkle and the desire to live. And that was how, from night to day, she left never to return, a decision made after hearing the tough words from her treating doctor:

—Mrs. Esmeralda, after three years of therapy, I'm in a position to discharge you, however, I must be very clear and honest, since your husband refuses to receive therapy, he is ill and will never change his actions, no matter how much he promises you and even your children, whom he claims to love very much but doesn't respect. You have two options: either you get a divorce or leave your house in a coffin.

Unsuccessful pleas, promises and cries of the wounded wolf went on for days, weeks and months without reaching the heart of Esmeralda, who would close that chapter of her life paying with a bleeding heart, without suspecting or having the slightest glimpse of the deep pain that was approaching and that she would never be able to overcome, because if she had known, she would have never gotten divorced, even assuming the risk that her life would be cut short by the hands of the one she swore to love and respect; Losing her children would be the karma she would carry to her grave.

Mario would prevent her happiness as a mother by taking her three children with astuteness and manipulation; Bearing in mind Esmeralda's suicide attempts caused by severe depression and being in psychiatric treatment, it was easy for him to obtain custody of the children granted by the court. Losing the right to live with her children, Esmeralda suffered a setback in her health treatment, became addicted to tobacco, smoked up to two packs of cigarettes a day, drank more than usual, stopped eating and became a wandering soul. She cried day and night nonstop; she walked miles and miles to her children's house, but they refused to see her. Devastated she became almost homeless; the support of an unconditional friend and a neighbor who fed her and took care of her during the nights of panic attacks, prevented her from falling and from giving in to Mario's pleas during the moments of weakness when she was willing to take it all back in order to recover the love of her children.

They say that time heals all wounds, apparently more than healing, it calms and clears the waters; everything settles allowing the facts to be seen more clearly, with the consequent regret and the wish that the events had been different and with a happy ending. In essence, relationships are complex, and more than that, human beings are.

In Todd's case, it could be simpler and perhaps time would heal his wounds with the arrival of a new dawn and the reunion of two soul mates, reason why Esmeralda firmly believed that once he regained lucidity and closed cycles, love would reign in their lives again. With those thoughts in mind, her answers were evasive, highlighting the wonderful aspects of the trip to Chile and the circumstances that had prevented them from fully enjoying the three months of vacation. Then she distanced herself a few meters and while chatting happily with a couple of friends on the phone, she was flirtatious, outlining her slim and beautiful silhouette, playing with her long hair and smiling, showing herself cheerful, happy and content. She didn't look at him for a single moment; knowing she was being watched by him, she strived to keep his attention captive. Her exuberant natural beauty, sparkling personality and attitude of independence and indifference, made him evoke their past in São Paulo, reliving the day of enormous delivery in which they made love over and over again .He thought he could feel the pleasure and hear the moans torn from her soul with the eruption of the seven orgasms of that day, which would forever be commemorated; that amazing and perfect carnal affinity, yes, how couldn't he not remember the eleven times with a record of seven orgasms in just one day. Wow, São Paulo, how couldn't he not remember what happened in that hotel room, with the embarrassment of receiving a warning note from the hotel management, asking for prudence and consideration towards the other guests, in particular, by those in adjoining rooms, who rather than applauding or being envious, were led by irritation to the reception to present their complaints. Esmeralda was hot-blooded, giving herself over to the passion of the art of loving with extreme care that burst spontaneously, making love with her hands, arms, legs, hair, eyes, mouth, with passion that erupted like a volcano. How not to make love again and again and as many times as possible that her body allowed, since years had passed since the last time Mario had made her see stars. The pain that his infidelities had caused her were so great that she had punished him with what hurt him the most, denying him the right to make her feel alive, avoiding reaching orgasm; punishing him by not allowing him to pump his chest out like a peacock, as a strong and virile man capable of sexually satisfying seven, and even more women, physically and economically, as he used to boast, saying that he should be an Arab, and even saying it to the treating doctor when Esmeralda was discharged, the only time he ever showed up at the clinic, with an air of bragging and thanking the doctor for recovering his wife's health, pointing out that now he was going to take her back home. Esmeralda hadn't taken into account that such a decision, to inhibit the culmination of the sexual act, would be so effective and irrevocable that it would end up damaging both and irreparably destroying their relationship; no specialists, competent doctors, sex therapists, medications, herbs and aphrodisiac foods, among them, the supposedly infallible recipe of seafood and raw garlic, aromatic candles, oils with which she covered her soft and delicate skin from head to toe, baths in the Jacuzzi and even nights of pool, were capable of reversing the fact that every time she climaxed and was on the verge of bursting into orgasm, there would be a thunderous void, like free falling, cooling everything in the blink of an eye. She asked for it, wanted it and worked psychologically hard for it, that she was never able to have an orgasm again. Mario felt furious, dissatisfied, moaned, shouted and howled like a wounded wolf, unable to make his wife happy in bed.

It was terrible for Esmeralda; they were years of doctor visits and even a couple of uterus and cervix surgeries, with no results. She began to distance herself from him, she asked to sleep in separate rooms, to which Mario flatly refused; he kept searching and demanding that she respond in bed, and by refusing, he had the perfect excuse to justify his affairs outside of their marriage. Years passed in her marital status as a divorced woman, without ever thinking about the subject, she had discarded it, as well as he idea of dating, until she met Todd, her Sweetheart.

From the first moment she heard his voice, her libido went through the roof; she felt sensual and attractive again, becoming interested for the first time, after the separation from Mario, in a new relationship. Several years had passed, twelve, to be exact, and in the first encounter with Todd she enjoyed the delivery with passion, but she couldn't reach an orgasm, despite feeling like she was about to explode; She attributed it to fear, to a guilty fear of feeling unfaithful and impure for giving herself to a second man. She reminded herself that she could only marry once and it was forever, respecting the tradition, teachings and good customs of conventional Chilean families. That first encounter, of three days, was an incipient delivery, a mixture of fear and self-consciousness, fueled by a nascent love that grew with enormous force, devoid of haste and demands. The fact of seeing each other again, hugging and feeling their warm closeness made them immensely happy, as they both had had a painful and rocky relationship; they shared getting to know each other a little more, despite the abysmal language barrier. He didn't speak any Spanish, and she only knew a couple of loose words in English. In a firm and very serious tone, he pointed out the difficulty they were facing:

—One of us has to learn the other language, either you learn English or I Spanish —immediately and without thinking or remembering the lousy ear she had for languages and music, like an innocent girl she raised her right index finger, and answered with firm determination:

—I will learn English!!!

110

–Really? Wow, that's fantastic, yes, excellent!!!

And so it was, as soon as she returned to Copiapó she enrolled in an academy and began English classes in the evening; classes from which she learned almost nothing, exhausted from intense days of work. It was almost impossible for her to resist the couple of hours of class, and even less retain the educational content, except for the teacher's jokes, which made her wake up and shake off her tiredness for a couple of minutes. She established an excellent relationship with her teacher, who offered himself as a matchmaker, and during a barbecue at Esmeralda's house, took advantage of inviting the candidate. The party was animated with all the guests present and the aroma of the barbecue could be smelled throughout the condominium; the professor, after seeing that the time was advancing, was concerned about the non-arrival of his candidate. He had promised Esmeralda that he was the perfect man, highlighting his attributes as a young gallant, handsome, gentleman and a very wealthy businessman. Mmmm, who could it be, she wondered without having the slightest interest in meeting him, but was curious. In that, he made his triumphant appearance on the terrace; He emerged smiling, entangled in the veils of the living room window holding a tray with salads, following the instructions of the matchmaker professor, yes, as if he were already the owner of the house. Esmeralda froze when she saw her friend Jacky's husband, although it was true that they were separated, they were still united in marriage. He didn't recognize her or pretend, or perhaps he didn't care that she was his ex's friend. Anyway, Esmeralda took the professor by the arm into the kitchen to reproach him for such an absurd idea. After a few years, Esmeralda told her friend about the incident and every time they remember they laugh.

Back home in London, back to everyday life, something very strange happened that favorably affected the couple's relationship: seeing Esmeralda work in her role as an executive woman, in charge of her dental and beauty clinic, fulfilling an extremely exhausting role due to the time difference and due to the fact of running a business that wasn't really her forte, seeing her so active, working long days that ended after midnight, the wonder occurred, her Sweetheart re-enchanted again; he helped her transform a guest bedroom into an office, where she installed an arsenal of file cabinets full of accounting information, contracts of all kinds and educational and scientific material. By assuming a role outside her skill set and work experience, in the absence of her daughter Renata, she was faced with the urgent need and the challenge of expressly venturing into the world of dentistry and aesthetic beauty, from learning about treatments, procedures, material and clinical dental instruments, to dealing with medical providers and administrative personnel; In short, everything that a health center needs in order to operate, that no matter how small, the laws and sanitary and tax requirements are the same as those of a large business conglomerate.

From time to time, Todd would pop by Esmeralda's office smiling. In a complacent and proud attitude, he watched her work with a smile from the door, in his eyes a sparkle of joy, admiration and love; He offered and prepared her coffee and even cooked her lunch and dinner. One morning he stopped to observe her as usual, for a few minutes, and then smiling he approached giving her a big kiss on the lips and with shimmering happiness confessed:

—I love that you're with me, that you live with me!!!

—Me too, I feel so happy by your side!!!

The honeymoon phase lasted a heartbeat; it would end as fast as it had started. Sedentary life, inactivity, and days of leisure would do their thing, except for brief daily walks through the park next to the house, and the month they went to the gym, when they returned from Chile. They had signed up at an incredibly interesting gym, equipped with all kinds of machines, personalized and group classes, ah, and the most extraordinary thing: opened 24 hours a day, from Monday to Monday. Since it operated on a 24/7 system, gym members had a card that allowed them to check in and out at any time they wanted, ideal for people who worked shifts and those who were sleep deprived or suffered from

113

insomnia. It was very nice to leave the house in the middle of the morning, walk through the park and cross the street to get to the gym. Todd did a two hours workout on the machines, and she spent one hour using the machines and the other hour in guided classes, such as body pump, yoga and aerobics. During their gym routine, two incidents occurred that caught Esmeralda's attention and one of them would be added to many others that were corroding the relationship. One morning, waiting for the traffic light to change to cross the street, a woman passed by on a bicycle; she and Todd looked at one another without greeting each other. Once the woman was out of sight, looking at Esmeralda seriously, he commented:

–That's the mother of my children.

–Ah, I barely noticed her, I only saw someone pass by on their bike.

–That was her –he added smiling.

–So, why didn't you greet one another?

–Noooo…for what? We don't even talk to each other, only on rare occasions. One time she went to my house… –she interrupted him raising her voice, and curiously asked:

–What? She went to your house?

–Yes, why do you ask? Are you jealous? –he innocently laughed and continued…

–Yes, she came to my house one time, when my children begged her to come visit me. Since she's a nurse, they wanted her to see me and convince me of going to the hospital because I was ill and my kids were worried and scared seeing me drunk every day, careless of my personal hygiene, delirious and vomiting blood…

–Ah, you were that ill?

–Yes, Elizabeth took me to the hospital. From time to time my ex and I run into each other on the street, because we live very close, but we don't say hello, we don't even look at each other. I'm not interested at all –he concluded with a sneer.

Effectively, she lived in the same neighborhood, at the other end, in a huge house with a beautiful front yard. One day he took her to see the house from the corner, with nostalgia and frustration he pointed at it, and murmured with his eyes reddened with fury:

–That's my house; I bought it for my children, to live in it with them, but… life was unbearable with their mother and when we broke up I left her the house so that my children could live comfortably and enjoy it. It was difficult for me to find another house to live in, it had to be close to my children, to be attentive to them and visit them. I told you how I spent more than six months in a hotel until I managed to find and buy the house where I live now. I regret not having bought the whole place...

—What do you mean? —she interrupte frowning.

—The basement isn't mine; I lost the great opportunity to buy it. It was just too much for me, although I could have leased it... but no... dealing with tenants is a tremendous problem... and now we're in trouble with the government regarding the change in legislation and the payment of taxes for the new appraisal...

—Ah, what a shame —Esmeralda added and continued—: the saddest part for me is not being able to use the backyard...

—Yes, that's true —he replied—, while for me, the most unpleasant thing is the hateful family that lives downstairs; they're unbearable, they complain about everything, about the noise, and not to mention the garbage...

The other event experienced at the gym that dented Esmeralda's heart and undermined the good relationship they were building, was something strange, to which she gave different interpretations. He would usually wait for Esmeralda to start her workout, and then he would sit on a machine far away from her, even if it was the same type, the ones that are generally placed one by the other. One day she saw him uncomfortable, nervously looking around, and ignoring her when she tried to ask if he was okay. Leaving the gym, he commented that he had seen a couple

116

of people he knew, friends of his son Johnny. On another occasion, the young man came over to say hello, they talked for a couple of minutes and Todd turned his back on Esmeralda, ignoring her. Indeed, he was trying by all means not to make his relationship with Esmeralda known. It hurt her deeply to feel denied in the eyes of those who knew him; she couldn't understand the reason for such an attitude. He was single, an independent adult, with no relationship to another woman; no matter how much she thought about it, she couldn't find the answer, and on the other hand, she remained youthful, beautiful and with a wonderful body for her almost sixty years of age, why would he be ashamed to be associated with her?

The relationship became colder and more distant every day, they shared brief conversations during mealtimes, and the rest of the day was spent on the coffee and milk-colored sofa, where both the silhouette of her body and her scents were tattooed and infused, testimonial traces of a sedentary lifestyle. They were years of sitting on the sofa, with his cell phone and tablet in his hands, and a few bottles of wine around, some empty, others half finished and others unopened. He remained faithful to the daily conversations with his journalist friend and the sick and endless messages with Maria; that inevitably took him back to his alcohol dependency. He promised Esmeralda that he wouldn't drink more than two bottles a day, and she in the meantime tried to drink more than usual to prevent him from drinking too much, and therefore finished each day drunk; absurd strategy that would quickly wreak havoc on her body and health. Meanwhile, he managed to sneak out to buy a few extra bottles, which he hid so that Esmeralda wouldn't see them, trying to make her believe that he was still drinking from the same bottle he had opened at lunchtime, while Esmeralda hid the new bottles to make him believe that he had already drunk them, replacing them with empty ones. It was a never-ending story, the game of cat and mouse that stressed Esmeralda so much.

The distance between them was more evident every day, the absence of expressions of love and living parallel lives under the same roof were the beginning of the end of their dreams to be fulfilled; left in the past would be the memory of that day when Esmeralda couldn't stop laughing for endless hours when listening:

–I'm single!!! –how not to laugh if her dream would become a reality, to marry her Sweetheart and be his first and only wife, a true privilege

–What? That means…that you're divorced, not that you're single. Ah!!!

–Noooo… no, I'm not divorced, I'm single, yes, I'm a single man; I've never been married to another woman.

118

Esmeralda interrupted him with a voice of interrogation, and with a look of deep curiosity she said:

—No way, I can't believe it; you're telling me that you've never been married, not even to the mother of your children?

—Yes, that's exactly what I'm saying. I never married the mother of my children.

Wow! It's just that she couldn't believe it or understand it; he looked so correct, so formal and respectful of English laws and traditions and of his native country, the United States. That was an improbable fact, at least for her, although fortunately it would facilitate her marriage, because she would never live with a man out of wedlock, it was something that wasn't in her essence as a peasant and traditional woman, who struggled to get rid of castrators and limiting peasant traditions, with the exception of getting married, that was a subject in which she couldn't compromise. She remembered that in one of the conversations with Terry, he told her that although it was true that he loved her with all the strength of his heart and wanted to live with her for the rest of his life, getting married was just a visa issue, otherwise he wouldn't have asked her to be his wife. She raised her voice and getting up faster than a sigh from the chair exclaimed:

—What are you saying? That you wouldn't have married me, that you did it just for the ridiculous visa?

—Yes, it's just that for me marriage isn't necessary, to live together you don't need to get married, in fact, every day there are fewer couples who get married.

—Ahhh, in my case, I would never live with a man without getting married, no, that doesn't go with me. We're just going to try and see, right? I'm not a commodity to try. It's all or nothing!!! I married for love and to make love, hahahaha.

—Hahahaha, great, I'm glad to know that you didn't marry me just to get a visa...

She interrupts him abruptly and blurts out:

—Way to keep insisting on the famous visa!!! How can you be so distrustful? I just can't believe it; I left everything for you, my life in Chile, my house, my job, my children, my family, my friends, everything, and you still have doubts about my love for you?

—Noooo, noooo, I didn't mean to say that, sorry. It's just that there are so many fake marriages, arranged just to get a visa to live here in England.

In reality, the visa issue in the United Kingdom is a real problem that worries the authorities, and it was probably one of the fundamental reasons for Brexit and its departure from the European Union. In fact, countless false couples and criminal gangs have been unmasked, dedicated to managing visas simulating couples in love, creating true love stories, consequently leading separate lives, and pretending they live in the same home; they have everything organized, not even the smallest detail escapes them in case they are supervised by Home Office staff, not only if it's a pink or blue toothbrush, but even menstrual pads and half-eaten chocolates. Well, as Esmeralda's life was a whirlwind of emotions and adventures, one day she received a call from a friend's friend, who claimed to be a lawyer and a real estate broker. He invited her to a coffee at his office to talk of Casa Chilena UK and of a good business plan that he wanted to propose. Characterized by her innocence, she went to the meeting at a luxurious hotel in Kensington. At the reception they informed her that they didn't know the person she was asking about, they offered her a seat and they served her a cup of coffee. After a few minutes the lawyer appeared, greeting her quickly and asking her to follow him. They left the hotel and like nothing he began the conversation, talking about trivialities on the way to his office. Esmeralda was perplexed and even afraid to continue, as she entered a narrow corridor between two buildings and up the stairs to a third floor. The office looked gloomy, messy, stacks of papers, blueprints and boxes scattered everywhere and even disposable coffee cups on the floor.

—Is this your office? You work here?

–Yes, sorry for the mess, I share the office with some colleagues and the cleaning lady hasn't come and to top it all off, we don't even have electricity. Today they're coming to repair some damages, if it wasn't for that, I would have offered you coffee.

Esmeralda was frozen, terrified, fearing the worst and thinking how she would defend herself against such a villain that had generated great doubts from the beginning; the appointment at a hotel where no meeting took place was the perfect strategy to attract the interest of any possible client, even more when it came to a simple person like Esmeralda, innocent and who always thought that these situations only existed in the movies. In short, the way he was dressed also caught her attention: jeans, shirt, sweatshirt and sneakers, nothing to do with the image of a businessman, and even less of a lawyer. She tried to maintain integrity and the thread of the conversation, sensing something off about him that she couldn't decipher; the atmosphere was tense, although he tried to show normality and security to his prey.

–So, tell me about yourself, I know that you're married and how you came to live in London; and what about children, do you have single daughters? …

She interrupts him:

—I don't understand why you invited me to your office, what business idea is it that you want to propose? Why do you ask me about my family and my children, and if I have single daughters? That has nothing to do with business.

—Ok, let' cut to the chase, I see that you're a woman not to be messed with, I like that.

—Yes, it's just that I don't have much time, I have other things to do, in fact, I'm going to meet a friend for lunch at a restaurant around here in this area —that wasn't true, she just wanted to convey that she was a woman who knew how to take care of herself and who had a support system.

—Ah, and is your friend single, pretty, young? —he asked in a sarcastic tone.

—What are you up to, looking for a girlfriend or doing business?

—Yes actually, I'm looking for single women, even better if they're single and don't have children.

—Ah, you know I have to get going… —says Esmeralda, at the same time grabbing her bag and getting up from her chair.

He gets up with her:

−Nooo, noooo, noooo, wait, you'll be interested; the business offer is that I need to find two women willing to marry in exchange for a large sum of money...

−Sorry, I don't understand... I really have to go; my friend is waiting for me.

−I'll tell you quickly, I have two clients, businessmen, who are desperate to settle in the United Kingdom, to facilitate and expand their businesses, and that is why they need to get married to obtain the UK visa...

−No, I really have to go, this isn't for me... −in that she reacted, she couldn't show rejection and even less criticize what he was proposing, or rather, what he actually did for work. So as not to upset him and avoid being attacked, she chose to go along with the conversation−: Sorry, I meant to say that I'm married; I'm not the person you're looking for...

He politely interrupted her and invited her to sit down again:

−You must know a lot of people and among them single women who live in England... right?

−Yes, I know a few people... but single women, mmmm, I don't think so.

−You can look, take your time...

−But I still don't understand, you want to find them wives?

–Yessss, yessss, you understood very well, and that's the business…

–What business are you talking about; we are talking about forming families…

–Not precisely, they would be arranged marriages just to obtain the visa. We take care of everything, photos, trips, hotels, the wedding, witnesses, a party and even the honeymoon and where they'll live; of course, it would be temporary, and in practice they wouldn't live a married life.

–Ah, nooo, I'm just stunned by how skillful you are at doing business, but finding "wives" seems very difficult…

–Nooo, it's not… everyone needs money; they would be paid £20 million and you would get a good commission.

–Mmmm, I appreciate the offer, however, the people I know are my age and older, almost all of them old…

–How about your daughters and granddaughters? It's a matter of finding out.

–Let me see and I'll let you know.

As soon as she managed to get out of the situation, she ran to the train station, deleted his contact, messages and calls, blocking any possibility of contact, leaving no trace of having known him because of the danger he represented, throwing it in the trash as an unfortunate experience or a bad dream.

Certainly, the difference in the level of education and social contact was an abyss with Terry, almost insurmountable in her relationship with him, not so much so with Todd, although for him it was and he made her feel it, she having lived in the countryside and being the daughter of a farm owner, attending Sunday masses, praying the rosary with her beloved grandmother Safira and not missing a single day of the Novena prayer for the month of Mary, the celebrations and events that Father Jose Maria led very well, and then his successor, Father Alcibíades Morales, accompanied by unconditional parishioners both in the parish of La Torina and in each hermitage of Mal Paso. She remembered very well Miss Mary, who lived in the parsonage and had raised a young girl with the priest who had been rescued from the clutches of death; she was a skinny and sickly girl. Her mother, not capable of caring for so many children, handed her over to the care of the priest and Miss Mary, but over the years, gossips commented that Sole was the daughter of the priest and Miss Mary, a fact almost impossible to determine, because by the size and bizarre way of dressing Miss Mary had, with long and puffy dresses and aprons, a possible pregnancy would have never been noticed. In short, Esmeralda's mother had always been very close with the priests, donating large amounts of food from the harvest of her father's farm, as well as fresh cheese and eggs from their chickens, turkeys for Christmas dinners and exquisite cakes that she baked to collaborate with raffles and bingos that they did to raise money for cancer patients, those with terminal illnesses, and families' victims of raging fires that reduced to ashes their homes and what little they had. Esmeralda, the daughter of a well-known Catholic family, liked to dress nicely, and stood out with her sisters among the other girls in town, known as the boss's daughters.

Instead, Terry dressed like a typical rock fan, in black, military-style high boots, leather jackets, and an infinity amount of t-shirts with devilish prints and skeletons, as well as his favorite t-shirts of famous rock bands with a photograph on the front and on the back the list of current tour concert venues. He didn't wear cloth shirts or pants. It was hard work for Esmeralda to gradually incorporate colored garments and for everyday use, and not to mention the moment when he had to accompany her to a ceremony, he hated wearing a suit nooooooooo, nooo, please, the tie bothered him so much that he felt like he was suffocating. Thanks to her charms, she even managed to dress him in a tuxedo so that he could accompany her to a gala dinner at the Lions Club to which she belonged and to dinner at the House of the British Parliament, but he left from the anniversary dinner of ACS, Anglo Chilean Society, because he didn't want to bow to Princess Anna;

despite respecting and defending the royal family, he didn't like the formality, he was a staunch enemy of protocols.

Todd dedicated himself to making his dream of moving to Italy come true. He spent days and nights in awe looking for dream properties in the Italian countryside. His desire was to move to Italy and live his old age there; he had the financial resources to do so and now he had Esmeralda to carry it out. His joy was overflowing; he shared with Esmeralda the preselected properties to visit, all huge mansions, provided with vast extensions of land and far from the big city. She looked at them as if she were inside the houses, making her appreciation known. In general, they were all beautiful old-fashioned houses, with towering walls that seemed to reach the sky, brick floors, and built on top of a mountain with a unique, spectacular view, exquisitely furnished according to the time of construction; fine taste in the décor and distinction made them more interesting and worthy of being considered in the list of properties to visit. Despite her amazement, none of them were to her complete satisfaction because of the distance from the city, about twenty to thirty kilometers away, without exaggeration. On the other hand, and despite the fact that she dreamed of living in a house like that, old, with thick walls, small windows and other large ones, brick floors and even stovetops for cooking and a fireplace in the rooms, she wanted to be surrounded by a neighborhood with people with whom she could share, practice Italian and soak up that wonderful culture, in addition to the fact that they would begin to age and each day would be more difficult for them to get around, drive and go shopping. With that near future in mind, more decadent than promising, in terms of life and health, she wouldn't trade the comforts of the big city for a life of hermits, a summer house yes, but to live, no. She dreamed of a bench outside her house to sit in the sun, greet every living soul that passed by, make thousands of friends, go to church and to the market and share with people; she wanted to be part of the community and its activities. He instead sought solitude, a contemplative life in the middle of nowhere. Esmeralda wasn't going to play Heidi, constantly singing the famous song from the cartoons that she had enjoyed so much with her siblings during her childhood: *Grandpa, tell me why I'm so happy...*, she selected a dozen wonderful properties, contacted the property agents and scheduled the house visits.

Although it's true that the spread of the Coronavirus in Italy was alarming, surpassing its own records and worse still, world records for infected cases and deaths per day, the pandemic hadn't reached the destination area, they remained without a single case; it was a matter of time. Todd, sitting in the corner of the living room, on his favorite sofa, personal and unique, with a privileged view of the street and the entrance door to the property, with an ideal light for reading, and warmed by the faint rays of sun that entered through the glass windows and through the cracks of the old and aged frames, which required urgent repair, he didn't worry about his surroundings, it wasn't something that kept him up at night. Attentive to the news, he updated Esmeralda:

—Today they reported a new case of Coronavirus in…

—Ah, what a pity, we won't be able to travel…

—But I'm going to travel no matter what, even if there are cases of COVID-19 in …

—But how? It's too dangerous, it's too risky…

—I don't care, nothing's going to happen to me, we are healthy people and where we're going to visit the properties, they're places far from the big cities, hundreds of kilometers from the epicenter of the infection. We are going to the north of Italy, we will visit Umbria, Lombardy, Toscana, Parrano, Perugia and Bettona, and the disaster is in the south of Italy, not the center or the north. I insist nothing is going to happen to us.

He commented smilingly, with confidence and trying to convince Esmeralda, to keep her away from fear and to be part of the trip; her company would be essential. He added in an enthusiastic and proud tone, due to the closeness of making his dream come true of buying a property and going to live in Tuscany:

—I have chosen fifteen properties to visit, we will rent a car and we will meet only with the representatives and agents of the brokerage in charge of the houses, and in some cases even with the owners and caretakers. We will have as little contact as possible with people, we will avoid eating in restaurants, we will eat in the house that I will rent, it is a very old house that easily dates from the 16th century; you will love it. Todi is an ancient city, very beautiful, with narrow streets, old buildings, and not to mention the temples built of stone, just like the small streets and alleys; wow, just like the fairytales. Ah, and since we'll have a car for personal use, we won't have to travel with the people who will show us the properties. So, as you can see, there's nothing to fear.

As a matter of fact, that's what they did; they left home and took a taxi to the airport. She always wore her face mask, while he refused to do so, only when it was an unavoidable requirement. They faced very contradictory situations regarding social distancing, the use of face masks and hand sanitizer. At Heathrow airport, in London, there was a very short line to check in. The airport was almost empty, it even seemed like ghosts were roaming. One or another bold, rather, intrepid, reckless passenger like them could be seen walking towards the airline counters, where they had to stand in line with a social distance of one meter

131

and wear a face mask; very rigorous security measures. Esmeralda, suffering from asthma, was in the category of patients exempt from wearing a mask, although she used it as long as breathing wasn't extremely difficult for her; On the other hand, she hadn't had time to go to the NHS, the British health service, to request the certificate that would allow her to make use of that exception, so she had to use it when required, despite being exempt. The anguish began to drown her when she thought that during the four-hour flight from London to Italy, she would inevitably have to wear the mask; and so, it was, although she was greatly surprised that the plane was basically empty, with only a few passengers. Arriving in Rome, at the Leonardo Da Vinci International Airport, they rented a car to travel to Todi, a medieval city where they would be staying, a journey that took approximately two hours. Both were amazed by the beautiful landscapes and the greenery of the meadows; they were enraptured by the mountains and the countryside, the crystal clear water and the turquoise color of the mighty rivers, canals and reservoirs, with gigantic bridges at an abysmal height that crossed from one end to the other, and the slopes of the mountain that surrounded them, with more than terrifying precipices of an exuberant beauty and without comparison. Esmeralda burst with joy and exaltation; she couldn't stop looking down the precipices and the top of the mountains, grateful for her magical red shoes and her Sweetheart who had made an effort to persuade her to accompany him.

The presence and obsession with Maria accompanied them throughout the trip to Italy. He spent a large part of his day sitting on the sofa in the apartment where they were staying in Todi; incredibly the same image was repeated as in his house in London, of staying for hours and nights on the sofa, in that strategic corner of the living room, next to the window, from where you could see the street and the entrance to the house, with his cell phone and tablet in hand. Being aware of this, Esmeralda suffered while ironing and cooking for him, at the same time that she implored God for the recovery of her great love and the liberation of the nightmares and the past that tormented him. He made her believe that he was reading the news and financial statements of the world, and in particular of the USA and the United Kingdom, but when he fell asleep after heavily drinking, she took on the Machiavellian task of reading his messages, which was very easy since he left his social media open: with Elizabeth they discussed the news from the USA and the United Kingdom, dismembering both presidents for their political behavior, criticism that lacked absolute veracity and objectivity as both were from the extreme left, while President Trump and Johnson represented the Conservative Party. On the other hand, the messages that he exchanged daily with Maria were about the same thing as always, reproaches and mutual criticism of his behavior, united by a stormy past, separated after she abandoned him in order to help her sister and at the same time taking refuge in her home in Switzerland. Esmeralda believed that once he managed to recover from alcoholism, his hallucinations, anxiety attacks and the severe depression he was in, everything would go back to the way it was before; thoughts and desires she held on to despite the harsh reality, thanks to the fact that she was a virtuous woman with admirable patience. But it wasn't only the shadow and presence of Maria, twenty years hadn't passed in vain, in addition to the fact that now, being able to communicate, they had realized that they had practically nothing in common, they had idealized their love based on misperceptions from both; they were united by an idyllic past of passion and false admiration of what each one had built, an ideal man, an exemplary father, an executive with a pure soul, idealistic, altruistic, of absolute self-sacrifice, of love and solidarity with others, while he saw in Esmeralda the ideal woman, well-travelled, an exemplary mother and impeccable professional. Once they faced reality, both speaking English, communicating optimally and after the trip to Chile, their souls were laid bear with reciprocal disenchantment.

Already in Italy, they began the tour of Umbria with the express objective of visiting the properties one by one; Esmeralda fulfilling a fundamental role as support and guide, assistant with technical equipment, internet, satellite navigator, food and everything required on the trip, use of face masks, etc. After a couple of days, the tension had built up to such a point that they decided to break up. She burst into tears, hiding her sadness and dignity, but kept it together and accompanied him in choosing a property. Two of the fifteen properties they visited really caught Esmeralda's attention, one of them built in a wonderful meadow, next to a stream that made her imagine paradise with the song of wild birds, the sound of the trees' leaves, the water gliding over stones, and small waterfalls with pools that invited you to take a dip, not to mention the fireplace, pool, terraces and gardens. The other property was like a museum and was very close to the city, also bordering the garden and the pool with a stream of crystal clear water, being the property what caught her attention the most, as it possessed a fragment of intact ancient architecture, a true millennial wealth that could easily be a piece of great admiration in a museum. As much as she insisted and suggested that he acquire one of them, in the end he decided on another property, one that Esmeralda didn't like at all, located in the middle of nowhere, 22 kilometers from the city and from the nearest house; it was filled with termites, which had been exterminated in the two lower floors, but not in the third or the attic. Nevertheless, it wasn't a difficult issue to overcome and accept, knowing that it wouldn't be her home. Despite this, they were very tough days for Esmeralda, accompanying him to choose the house of his dreams so that he could share it with another woman, probably Maria or a new one. She was more tormented by the tragic ending of her great love, a love she had dreamt of and idealized above all reality. She tried to occupy her mind enjoying the majestic landscape of

Tuscany, the impressive landscapes of the routes between one property and another, and even more when moving to different locations in northern Italy. She loved Umbria, a land of dreams even more for her since she was a nature lover, having been born and raised in the countryside. Esmeralda became an ace in practicing resilience mechanisms and resuming the process of experiencing detachment, taking advantage of her journey and ceasing the feeling of being used, was her salvation so as not to succumb to the despair of mourning such an announced ending. It was a process that despite all the pain and suffering, hadn't been so difficult because it made her open her eyes, since, devoid of dreams and idealism, she realized that they weren't made for each other and that she had been used, that he tended to use people, probably unconsciously, because he was accustomed to having staff at his service since he was a child, and later in his working life; yes, it most likely was unconsciously, having that behavior so ingrained in his personality.

At the end of 2019, the first cases of COVID-19 were detected in the United Kingdom, and just four months after the start of the pandemic, the British were shaken with the shocking message from the Prime Minister, Boris Johnson: ... "With much pain and regret, we will see the departure of very close people, family and friends, who will lose their lives as a result of the COVID-19 pandemic. It is estimated that over 20,000 people will die in the

UK as a result of the Coronavirus. We must take care of ourselves, protect ourselves, follow the instructions of our health authorities and avoid leaving our homes, and only do so if it is strictly necessary" ...

The return from Rome to London became anguishing due to the uncertainty caused by the closure of airlines and airports. As a result of the uncontrolled increase in infections and deaths, governments began to close borders as a health strategy to prevent the spread of the pandemic, because in particular, passengers were the transmission vehicles of COVID-19 and the new variants product of virus mutations, from one territory to another. Hearing and seeing the news was chilling, terrifying images coming specifically from Italy and Spain, with absolutely empty streets, depopulated cities, trucks transporting thousands of bodies of victims of the pandemic, buried in mass graves without the goodbye from their relatives or their closes ones, due to the risk of contracting the virus and increasing the numbers of sick and deceased, being the first two European countries most affected by the resounding spread of the virus.

New cases began to be reported in different parts of the world with the pandemic, and case zero was quickly notified in other countries in Europe, including the United Kingdom. Months later, the virus would reach South America, via tourists who had been on vacation in countries where the Coronavirus was already present, an expected and inevitable fact, no matter how much the governments, together with their health advisors, public health professionals and pandemic experts, tried to avoid it; or like the mayor of a commune in the small north of Chile, who decreed the closure of its border, preventing the access of all vehicles and people, whether by land, air or on foot. As a public health worker, she was certain that closing the community would prevent the pandemic by not allowing the virus access. However, the north of Chile is a territory of vast desert, so as soon as the measure was announced, people began to move, both entering and leaving, through alternative paths and new accesses to the open field, in addition to the fact that the building authority received a superior order from the competent government agency, instructing to cancel the mobility restriction of people in the port commune because it was out of their hands; they went to court to appeal but didn't get the order.

Other health authorities and scientists pointed out that it was necessary for the entire population to be infected with the virus to obtain herd immunity. That was the case in Sweden, where the strategy was implemented, and even the UK government announced it as a policy to curb the pandemic, and hundreds of scientists disagreed. Skeptics of the pandemic also emerged, flatly denying its natural existence, denouncing and complaining that it had been created in a laboratory and that through vaccines the entire population would be controlled by means of a microchip that would enter the body through the vaccine. Meanwhile, the World Health Organization (WHO) was categorical in stating: "Letting people contract COVID-19 to achieve herd immunity is not a strategy, it's a tragedy".

Another theory emerged, which asserted that it was a strategy to reduce the overpopulation, infecting people so that the weakest would die, including the elderly, sick and most vulnerable; a natural cleanse of population. While children wouldn't be infected by the virus as they have their own immunity. That is how, from the notification and publication of the first cases of COVID-19 by the health authorities led by the World Health Organization, currents of opposition and detractors of the health alert arose worldwide, speaking of a "Plandemic" structured for economic purposes and population control by elitist groups with great economic power, and among them they mentioned Bill Gates.

In March 2020, just a few months after the start of the Coronavirus pandemic, the first positive effects of the health crisis were beginning to be perceived; just as the virus had brought despair to the world in many ways, it had also generated acts of kindness. Difficult times were evidenced for the planet as the Coronavirus continued to spread. The number of infected and deaths were increasing day by day; many cities and even countries were under quarantine, and millions of people were forced to isolate themselves. However, amid all the worrying news, there was also reason for hope. Among them, the positive effects on the environment, such as the decline in environmental pollution levels. As countries went into quarantine due to the virus, significant drops in contamination levels were recorded. The reduction of movement in large cities caused direct effects on the environment, such as the decrease in the emission of pollutants into the atmosphere and the increase in the generation of domestic and hospital waste. China, like northern Italy, showed major drops in levels of nitrogen dioxide, a toxic gas that severely contaminates the air, amid reduced industrial activity and fewer car trips, thanks to the mandatory lockdown of the entire population. Researchers in New York also told BBC that according to preliminary results, carbon monoxide, mainly produced by cars, was reduced by almost 50% compared to the previous year in that US city; And with airlines canceling flights in masse and millions of people working from home, it was expected for the tendency to follow this downward path. In a similar case, the residents of Venice, Italy, noticed a great improvement in the water quality of the famous canals that cross the city: they returned to having crystal clear waters, recovering their transparency due to the little movement of boats, motorboats and gondolas. The canals of popular tourist destinations in northern Italy were empty amid the virus outbreak, which had allowed sediment to accumulate at the bottom of the canals; the water, which was usually murky, had become so clear that you could even see fish. On the other hand, social sensitivity and generosity went beyond the horizons of family, friends and neighbors, generating signs of solidarity even with unknown people, surpassing reactions of hysteria and collective anguish due to unrestrained purchases and fights over toilet paper and canned foods; but the virus also spurred acts of kindness around the world.

Two New Yorkers gathered 1,300 volunteers in 72 hours to deliver food and medicine to elderly and vulnerable people in the city; Facebook said hundreds of thousands of people in the UK joined local support groups set up to combat the virus, while similar groups formed in Canada. Supermarkets in various corners of the planet, from Argentina to Australia, created a special "senior hour" so that older people and those with disabilities could shop in peace, avoiding crowds and reducing the risks of contracting the virus; a strategy that was adopted in various countries around the world, including the United Kingdom. Many people also donated money, shared food and dessert recipes, and ideas on how to exercise at home; some sent messages of encouragement to seniors self-isolating, and transformed businesses into food delivery centers. Another commendable initiative to raise money was the campaign promoted by British Captain Sir Tom Moore, a World War II veteran, his optimism was contagious; He inspired the entire United Kingdom in those difficult times of the pandemic.

At 99 years old, he decided he was going to walk every day until he reached 100 laps in his garden, before he was 100 years old. His goal was to raise £1,000 to benefit service workers on the front lines of the NHS, the British National Health Service, in the battle against COVID-19 and he managed to raise £33 million.

The trip back to London was chaotic, consequently due to the fact that the airlines had begun to suspend flights and everyone was struggling to get back home, and with overbooked flights it was impossible to comply with the protocols to prevent the spread of COVID-19. Esmeralda protected herself during the flight and the journey from the airport to her house by wearing a face mask, but not Todd, who was reluctant to do so, even though they weren't required on the flight. In the back row where they were seated, a female passenger coughed throughout the entire flight, and most passengers traveled without wearing masks. There was no doubt in mind that this was where Esmeralda and Todd contracted the Coronavirus.

Back in London, both were faced with living under the same roof during the fifteen-day quarantine imposed by health and government authorities on anyone who entered the United Kingdom from a country with COVID-19; a tense and uncomfortable situation, after their mutual agreement to definitively end their relationship. He moved into the guest room, leaving her the main room. The relationship grew more distant every day, becoming colder and unbearable. Esmeralda no longer saw in that man the synthesis of passionate love that she had seen at some point in her life; she was beginning to see him as he really was: a selfish, egotistical person without an ounce of empathy in his body towards others.

In spite of this, she, with an attitude out of character as a strong and empowered woman, made the last attempts to recover the relationship, while he resumed his life, without abiding by any of the safety regulations; he refused to wear a face mask, alluding to the fact that there was nothing to worry about, that it was just a new form of influenza and that, thanks to the technological development of Great Britain, there wouldn't be a shortage problem, and even less of basic products and medicines, water and fuel.

Todd's daily routine, during the COVID-19 pandemic and quarantine period, before traveling to Italy and upon his return, was to go to the express supermarket located four blocks from his house, to buy two, three and even more bottles of white wine or whatever they had in stock. He was already so immersed in alcoholism that nothing mattered to him, and any drink even the cheapest and the worst quality, was good enough for him. He did this every day and without any issues, really; He took advantage of the occasion to buy some food, fruits and vegetables, meat and sometimes ice cream for Esmeralda. However, upon returning from Italy he would no longer indulge her whims, even knowing that ice cream was Esmeralda's weakness, that she devoured it whether it was winter or summer, cold or a rainy day; And, of course, he also acquired the inevitable toilet paper, which was never lacking despite the fact that some people bought too much of it. For him, this showed that, although the shelves weren't full like usual, food wasn't scarce, and even though some things were missing, the most basic was available, since it wasn't permitted to buy more than one unit of each product per person.

Esmeralda managed to prepare food for both of them. They ate normal portions for lunch, and in the middle of the afternoon he would uncover the pots in the kitchen and devour what was left, not caring if it was cold; and, of course, at dinner time there was only enough for one serving. Esmeralda, in spite of everything, would warm it up and offer it to him sweetly, commenting that she wouldn't have dinner that night, generally alluding that her stomach hurt or that she wasn't hungry. He, without thinking about her, ate everything between drinks, without even considering that perhaps she did want to have dinner. The change in Todd was incredible, he had lost his good table manners, in fact, he no longer sat at the dinner table to eat, instead preferred to do so on his sofa with the plate in his hand; many times, he ate with his fingers, without a fork and knife, not even taking the time to heat up the food in the microwave.

It takes a lot of love to overcome those things, and unfortunately, she had realized that love began to be missing in the relationship. That knowledge had hit her right on the face, in the midst of the mandatory confinement and quarantine period that prevented her from going out in search of help, of a new shelter where to take refuge and start a new life.

After leaving her husband, Esmeralda chose to break all ties and communication with him, except in unavoidable circumstances, such as when she had to go to the offices of the Chilean consulate in London to sign the divorce papers, because she wanted to get a divorce as soon as possible to recover her freedom and marry her beloved Sweetheart, in addition to the fact that due to her upbringing of a traditional peasant and macho family, living together out of wedlock was unthinkable.

It was a difficult time for both; the first encounter after almost two months took place on Christmas Eve and prior to the trip she would take without him to her beloved Chile. His reddened eyes, dull and full of tears, about to burst in a flow of infinite sadness, portrayed the deep sorrow and pain for the loss of his beloved Esmeralda, while she was invaded by feelings of guilt and remorse, typical of the macho culture in which she had been raised, traditions and prejudices that she tried to get rid of. Esmeralda felt stunned and guilty, being literally the bad guy in the movie, the unfaithful woman who had left home and a good man, a husband

145

without vices, homebody and affectionate; what more could she have asked for, what more could she aspire to, transformed into a vile floozy, who gave free rein to her lust and unbridled passion to run into her lover's arms. Those were the dark thoughts that haunted her subconscious, tormenting her; they went round and round in her head, about to explode. She avoided his gaze, she couldn't look into the eyes of the man who was still her husband, and to whom she was united by a great feeling of love and infinite gratitude. In her desperation and anguish, ideas arose that were impossible to put into practice, like living with both of them; flashes of rescue lights in the midst of that storm.

The consulate staff showed a compassionate attitude towards her and repudiated the Englishman's actions, at least that's what she thought she perceived in the body language of those who showed unsuccessful efforts for more details. The consul even called her to his private office, to sign in his presence the document that formalized the beginning of the rigorous divorce proceedings, signatures that, although must be made in person before the certifying officer, in that case the consul, in reality was signed before the chancellor; in short, not even the diplomats were exempt from curiosity. The consul detained her for more than twenty minutes, inquiring about details of the relationship, the reasons for the separation, what would happen to her life from now on, if there would be an imminent return to Chile or if she would remain in the United Kingdom, where she would live, how she would financially support herself; In essence, a thousand and one questions that weren't relevant to the signing of the documentation. Perhaps Esmeralda should have appreciated the consul's consideration, concern and deference given her closeness to the Chilean authorities in the United Kingdom, due to her condition as former president of Casa Chilena UK, but no, it was merely the curiosity of an old woman, to which Esmeralda was absolutely oblivious. She repudiated hearing that in social gatherings they touched on personal subjects that were none of anyone's business, even more so when the person in question wasn't present, and when faced with this type of situation, she would immediately change the subject; if her opinion was required, she would simply smile or respond hoping everything was fine and that it wouldn't go beyond being misunderstandings.

When saying goodbye, Terry tried to hug and press Esmeralda against his chest, wanting to hold her close to him. She escaped and remembered the moment when, for the first time, he was about to kiss her, but she dodged it by quickly escaping downstairs in one of the most complex train stations in the British capital, as Bank Station is, where it is habitual for the English to even get lost in the labyrinth, tunnels, platforms and crossroads of stations.

The second encounter was requested by him to sign the documents related to the famous shared vacation plan, to which she had convinced him of joining; a plan that after a few months, they retracted considering that it was a big scam when verifying that of the thousand and one wonders that they offered, it was practically impossible to access even a tenth of them for a many reasons or excuses: whether it was the restrictions, the lack of seniority, the points, the availability of dates; it was and continued to be a subject of discord due to the high sum of money that had to be disbursed each month and without receiving any benefits. At the moment of making the decision to cancel the plan, it was impossible unless the total contract was canceled, which had been signed for life, meaning... the fine print was financially lapidary, and despite being a topic that brought them discord, the encounter was jovial and almost funny.

Terry offered her whiskey and she refused to let him pay, considering that it wasn't his duty and bearing in mind that she was no longer his wife; they agreed to pay a round each, as is customary in British culture: friends meet up at a bar, the first one buys drinks for everyone, then the second round is paid by another friend, and so on. The issue is when groups are very large, which happens frequently, and it isn't possible to drink ten beers, let alone ten whiskeys, even worse when they are double whiskeys, as was the case with Esmeralda, although there was never a lack of *a fish* – A fish: expression used to refer to someone who drinks a lot without changing countenance, as if it were water, and in reality there was never a lack of fish, as in the case of a couple of existing fish in his close circle of friends: Paul and David. In essence, the conversation had been pleasant until it was time to do the math: no, not for anything in the world would he accept that Esmeralda would receive fifty percent of the profit from the trial in the supposed case of winning, as the trial lawyer had assured them. He became angry, his face reddened, his eyes seemed to throw flames, and his voice became loud, aggressive, and inquisitive. In the end, Esmeralda gave in to part of the requirements, managing to calm the waters. That day, he did manage to kiss her on the lips, catching her off guard. She didn't respond, but did enjoy it.

After the trip to Chile, living with Todd became suffocating and unbearable. In spite of everything, they insisted and traveled to Italy. Those days were a parenthesis in their stormy relationship, although she knew in the depths of her soul that things with her Sweetheart could no longer be put back together. She felt sadness, spite, nostalgia, a deep pain that didn't allow her to breathe and she even, perhaps unconsciously, clung to the possibility of recovering her great love.

When they returned to normal life and decided that it was no longer possible to live together, Todd, in a plaintive tone and with the air of a Good Samaritan, announced:

—While you look for a place to live, you can stay as long as you need. You don't have to worry; you will always have a plate of food and shelter here.

Esmeralda bit her tongue and walked upstairs, almost running, to bury her head in a pillow like a true ostrich in the sand. She burst into tears trying to placate the frustration and anger of the humiliation that his words of compassion caused her.

But things got complicated with the Coronavirus and the mandatory confinement.

The day that Esmeralda met up with Terry at the park, already infected with the Coronavirus, she let Todd know that she would get together with a friend who would help her find a place to live. He wished her the best of luck and reminded her that there was no rush, reiterating that she could stay as long as she needed until she found a place to move. Those kinds of comments made her blood boil with rage; it was like receiving a fatal blow, a saber pierced into her indomitable soul of reckless personality and, above all, of an empowered, independent and free woman. She wouldn't tolerate causing pity and even less receiving crumbs. She needed to leave as soon as possible, in a dignified manner and, above all, avoiding stressing the relationship even more and invading his privacy, knowing Elizabeth and Maria were close by, although thanks to the pandemic they couldn't visit each other, but he didn't care about complying with the regulations imposed by the government and the health authorities; so surely he wouldn't refuse any visit, and of course, even less from Maria.

Esmeralda said goodbye carrying a backpack filled with a couple of changes of clothes and personal hygiene supplies, in addition to her medication. She set off at a steady and determined pace to meet Terry, who had invited her to spend the weekend together, although she wasn't entirely sure. At midnight that day, the UK-wide lockdown announcement came into effect, which precipitated events… After being certain that she wouldn't return home that night, she sent Todd a message letting him know that she would be staying at her girlfriend's house.

They were overcome with a mixture of nervousness and fear on the train ride to his house, despite having made the decision with maturity and being certain that love united them, it was inevitable for her to feel guilty and he with a broken heart. The house looked tidy and smelled fresh, which emanated from the beautiful roses that he had bought for Esmeralda, flowers that she thanked with a kiss and a hug of infinite sweetness and love. They were alone; he made sure that his son Connor was staying at his fiancée's house for the weekend. They had a light meal, a couple of drinks to the beat of the music, holding each other, and enjoying each other's company and love. It was inevitable not to burst into tears after making love… The following week, she returned to Todd's house for her personal belongings and car, violating the ban on leaving the house; she was accompanied by Terry who was waiting for her a block away to avoid the encounter, because supposedly she had moved into her girlfriend's house. Todd smilingly received her with a kiss on the cheek, offered her coffee, which she gladly accepted, and while he prepared it, she went to the bedroom to get her clothes. With haste and nervousness, she packed two suitcases and a few bags with clothing, personal accessories and books, luggage that complemented an infinity amount of boxes and bags that were waiting for her in the entrance hall of the house, which he had diligently prepared to facilitate the work. With both cars, Terry's and hers, packed to the roof, she headed back to her home as a married woman. The farewell with Todd was cordial, they were grateful for the opportunity that each had offered, the time shared, and, above all, they said goodbye on good terms, recognizing and accepting that their lives had different directions, after verifying that the fire of passion that united them in the past had been completely extinguished, love of which not even ashes remained.

They agreed that, once the quarantine was over, she would remove the rest of her furniture and belongings, however, and after a week, the commitment had become unknown to Todd, who sent her repeated emails and WhatsApp messages demanding that she immediately remove the rest of her things from his property or he would throw them out on the street. Esmeralda, aware that he was capable of doing so, and given the impossibility of going out due to the forced confinement and because of her extremely serious state as she was suffering acute symptoms of COVID-19, she begged him to wait, promising that as soon as she felt better she would get her things; despite being in quarantine, she would once again break the rules risking being sanctioned and fined in the event that the police stopped her, in order to accede to his request and avoid having her belongings suffer the same fate as Maria's. He insisted that she had to get her things immediately because the existence of women's clothing and personal belongings in his house affected his independence and privacy; he insisted recklessly and ironically, announcing that he was going to rebuild his life and she would be complicating the situation by not wanting to remove her things from his house. In the end he reluctantly agreed to wait just a week, blurting out:

—If you don't get your things in the stipulated timeframe, I will throw them out on the street.

Faced with that intransigence, and despite her serious health condition, she was forced to rent a moving truck, which he had fraudulently managed by breaking the confinement restrictions. She did her best to get up from her sickbed while Terry was at work, because if he had been home, he would have stopped her. Esmeralda drove her car with great difficulty, exhausted, without strength, adding the stress of breaking quarantine, and crossing

London from one end to the other. Upon arrival, although they kindly greeted each other, the visit was short and tense; Opportunity in which she cunningly made one last move of revenge. She invited him to uncork a bottle of champagne that she had among her belongings, to toast the farewell, generating the perfect occasion for a couple of suggestive and compromising photographs of them making a toast and others taken in the bedroom, taking advantage of the moment when she went upstairs to get her coat from the back of the closet; Photographs that she then published on her Facebook and other social media, to irritate and make Maria jealous, who was very attentive to the details of the relationship. They were photographs that would make their relationship appear to be excellent, irrefutable proof of them living together, although he would flatly deny his relationship with Esmeralda, and not only of the breakup, but also of ever being together in the distant and recent past. And that's how Esmeralda received an email from Maria, who was apparently her follower and number one fan, inquiring about the details of the relationship and wishing her the greatest happiness, emphasizing that she was backing out, getting out of the way for them to fully enjoy their love. Meanwhile, Todd's emails and WhatsApp messages were of unbridled fury and rage, cursing her existence and the fact that she had crossed his life. On the other hand, Esmeralda's attitude was reproached by close friends, and even her mother called her attention, who didn't understand what was happening and what she was showing on social media.

Todd also suffered from the Coronavirus, and once he recovered, made his dream of moving to the Italian countryside come true, where he would spend the rest of his life in the faithful company of alcohol and his ghost friends.

Back with Terry, Esmeralda blossomed again, radiating light and happiness as she felt queen of her home, enjoying the garden, eating healthy and, above all, having the certainty of loving and being fully loved, along with the relief of having definitively closed the circle of love that had kept her fancifully tied and clinging on to Todd. Living in joy, peace and serenity, she thanked God for his infinite mercy and indulgence. Today, she not only loved Terry, she also admired his infinite kindness, his ability to forgive and forget and, above all, his unfailing love.

This happiness was abruptly altered with the sudden onset of acute symptoms of a COVID-19 infection. Esmeralda presented increasingly intense respiratory problems that made it difficult to breathe, symptoms accentuated by a persistent cough, generalized pain in the body and a state of general exhaustion, in addition to an intense headache, dizziness, chills, sweating and insatiable thirst. They went to a health care center where they took the COVID-19 test, and pending the result of the PCR –PCR: an acronym in English that means Polymerase Chain Reaction, a diagnostic test that allows detecting a fragment of the genetic material of a pathogen, in this case, the COVID-19 virus– she was instructed to maintain a strict quarantine, resting and drinking plenty of fluids, as well as continuing to take her asthma medications and using inhalers more frequently if necessary, and in the event of difficulty breathing or worsening symptoms, she had to immediately go to the emergency room of the nearest hospital or request an ambulance service.

The next day, she received a call from the NHS informing her that she was indeed infected with the Coronavirus, the PCR test had come back positive for COVID-19. They ordered her to pickup her medication from a specific pharmacy, to strictly administer according to the indications, and if she got worse, intubation to an artificial respirator would be necessary in a hospital that had availability of mechanical equipment; It was important to keep in mind that there was an excess demand and the fact of being treated in a health center implemented to treat COVID-19 patients didn't necessarily mean that she would receive the required treatment of being intubated. Esmeralda immediately went to her medical friends who specialized in bronchopulmonary diseases, her treating doctor in Santiago de Chile, and her friend Lorenzo in Bergamo, Italy, who despite being overloaded with work, providing services on the front line in a public health hospital complex, the epicenter of COVID-19 cases, helped her by providing medical advice through the phone, committing to calling every day to follow her evolution and indicating the procedures to follow. Ah, regarding the pandemic, he commented that the health situation was extremely critical; they didn't have enough staff or beds and even less the respiratory equipment needed to respond to the growing demand; the cases were endless. He concluded by wishing her the best of luck and a fast recovery.

The Coronavirus pandemic and confinement brought Terry and Esmeralda together; they spent day and night together, except when he was working, they prepared different meals, they made use of the right to go for a walk one hour a day, they enjoyed the park, the rain and the sunny days. They had fun playing board games, cards and watching movies, they also spent hours gardening and growing vegetables, as a precautionary measure in case of a food shortage caused by the pandemic. They enjoyed eating delicious tomatoes, green beans, Swiss chard, potatoes and strawberries, in addition to medicinal herbs, products from their home garden that were part of their fresh and nutritious diet, ideal for strengthening the immune system. They also built a chicken coop with recycled pallet wood materials; through a chicken protection shelter and social media, they got their supplies of birds, which were raised and cared for as pets. Each hen was given a name and responded to the call of their masters, and were hand fed. The king was Condorito, a Peking rooster that had been a gift from a family that had traveled from Oxford to London to deliver the first pet of the family, and because they were pets, they only made use of the eggs.

Like a large part of the families in quarantine, they took advantage of the time to tidy and repair the house, clean closets, cellars and even the attic, getting rid of countless things that they had kept for years; many others in good condition, were donated to charity which then sold the items to raise money to help finance their social services with cancer patients, organ transplants, orphaned children, the elderly, war veterans, among other philanthropic works. The free time as a result of the confinement gave Esmeralda the opportunity to dedicate herself to her passion for writing. Since she was a child she had had the ability to express herself through words. She wrote short stories, tales, poems and even songs as a hobby, and thanks to the pandemic she had time to write and finish her first novel published on Amazon and which reached the position of best seller for sales record during the first weeks after its publication, a novel that she titled *The Pilgrim Bride. Is a second marriage better than the first?* In addition, she took a meditation course that allowed her to improve her mental health, so deteriorated by the confinement, the marital crisis and the detachment from her children and even from her famous melted Sweetheart.

There were good, bad, and terrible things during the pandemic and significant gains for the world when it came to family's being together. For example, parents had the opportunity to stay full time with their children, days and nights, seeing how they spent their days taking online classes, fulfilling their role of co-educators, and discovering the abilities, skills and also weaknesses in their children's development, particularly in the school environment. On the other hand, mandatory confinement, sharing 24 hours a day for weeks and months, in small spaces and some without access to a garden or balcony, made it difficult for interpersonal relationships between family members and those who shared the same home, intensifying incompatibilities and differences, and accentuating family discussions. Caregiver burnout syndrome was also generated, not only of children, but also of elders; caring for patients with degenerative disorders and dealing with young adolescents resulted in the dissolution of couples, while some became stronger and others reconciled; new relationships also arose and the number of family members even increased. Just as some couples chose different paths, others, on the other hand, were reacquaint during the pandemic, as had happened to Esmeralda herself. The most surprising and atypical cases of human relationships discovered and others disclosed, were of people who believed they were heterosexual, and who even had a spouse of the other sex and children, and out of the blue started a new relationship with a person of the same sex, as had been the case with Ale, a friend of Esmeralda, who at the beginning of the pandemic publicly declared:

"Here we all take care of each other and support each other, some will fight, separate, others will marry, divorce and even reconcile, but we will ALL make it out of here alive". And today the famous Ale is happily married to a beautiful young lady, hard to believe, after she had loved men and couldn't live without them.

Esmeralda was faced with the dilemma of whether or not to get vaccinated against Covid-19; after the vast amount of information with which she was bombarded daily and circulated on social media, generating uncertainty not only for her, but for millions of people worldwide. It was information that her husband alluded to categorically refuse to be inoculated, he wouldn't allow it under any circumstance; a man of unbreakable health and reluctant to take medicine, he decided not to do it. Esmeralda, after going over and over the pros and cons, adhered to Terry's determination by also opting not to get vaccinated, although an unavoidable problem arose that made them hesitate: entering certain places, venues and public access sites, from health establishments, to supermarkets and entertainment centers, where they not only required the use of face masks and hand sanitizer, but now the entrance was subject to presenting the vaccination certificate against Covid-19.

Faced with this scenario, although it caught her attention and worried her, wasn't a big issue since she thought she could avoid it, but when a second dose was necessary, the panorama became more complex, until she reached a crisis when her magical and wonderful red shoes came to her, very smiling and euphoric:

–Esmeraldaaaaa... Esmeraldaaaa... we are ready to travel – they repeated over and over again, while they fluttered smilingly around her body, pretending to be an airplane.

–Yessss, it's time to travel –she responded even more euphoric than her magical red shoes with a smile from ear to ear.

But the joy completely vanished when remembering that to travel abroad it was required to be vaccinated with both doses. She replied regretfully:

–I'm sorry, my wonderful red shoes, we won't be able to travel just yet. Let's wait for the pandemic to end, surely in a couple of months.

Her innocence led her to believe that the pandemic would end as fast as it had started, without suspecting at all that it would last more than two years in its critical manifestation, with three waves of variants resulting from virus mutations, and more than that, it had come to stay. At that moment, her magical red shoes reappeared, in a cheerful and mischievous tone that refreshed her mind and heart:

161

—Excuse me, my darling, what about the arrival of your new little grandson?

—Oh, yessss… right, we have to travel to Australia to accompany my son Apollo in the birth of his firstborn. Yes, we are going to travel.

Esmeralda experienced the emotion and joy of seeing herself together with her son and with her new grandson in her arms; however, at the same time she was prey to anguish and concern as she evoked the moment of childbirth and the circumstances in which Apollo had been born: premature, with health difficulties that kept him hospitalized in an incubator and underwent surgery three times. Nevertheless, she knew that the situation was fortunately different; the baby was healthy as confirmed by medical tests and ultrasound. Her magical red shoes appeared again:

—Esmeralda, will we also have to get vaccinated and get the PCR test?

—Hahahahaha! What nonsense are you talking about? Now get out of my sight, it's not time to travel yet.

—Heyyyy, heyyy, but you will have to get vaccinated… hahahahaha!

–Noooo… I won't get vaccinated, that's decided; I won't get vaccinated. Or do you want me to die? …

Abruptly she reacted once again when realizing that in order to travel abroad, both when leaving and returning from a trip, whether by land, sea or air, it was a fundamental requirement to present the vaccination certificate, and not just a vaccine against COVID-19, it was required to have both doses, a negative PCR test, mobility pass and quarantine upon arrival and when returning from other countries… Uuufffff! It was a true ordeal of paperwork, vaccines and tests.

She felt like the world was caving in… No way, there was no other way out, she would have to get vaccinated against her will, because her family is her family, and no CORONAVIRUS was going to stop her from the adventure and pleasure of traveling!!!

That is how Esmeralda and Terry, who weren't easy to convince, voluntarily agreed, despite grumbling, to go to a vaccination center in order to be inoculated with two vaccines against COVID-19. The effects of the first dose produced reactions of great concern and discomfort in both, particularly in Esmeralda, who presented fever, intense headache and muscle pain, and exhaustion; it was horrible, it was like reliving the acute days of the illness, but fortunately the symptoms gradually diminished until they disappeared after a week. The effects of the second dose were milder and of short duration, however, as the concern remained latent in relation to possible adverse reactions, and being aware of countless cases of patients who had even died after being inoculated, she did the test of placing a coin in the area of the arm where she had received the vaccines, and horrified she verified that it presented magnetization; the coin was attracted and remained attached to her arm, thus verifying the information disclosed on social media by the detractors of the pandemic and who rejected getting vaccinated. She was shocked to see that what was being said against the massive vaccination campaign of the world population was indeed partly real.

As life is usually difficult and the road is paved in stone, sometimes, thankfully not always, despite having the vaccines, there were countries that didn't authorize the entry or exit of people, this being the case of Australia that made it impossible for both her and Lidia's mother, Lidia being Apollo's wife, to accompany their children in such an important and significant event in their lives as was the arrival of their child. Apollo and Lidia received, in a very distant land and in the absence of their loved ones, the arrival of their firstborn Renato, a robust and healthy baby, on September 23, 2021, in the midst of a pandemic. Yes, their grandson Renatito was born in times of pandemic.

Little by little, the cases of people infected with the Coronavirus decreased and with this the number of hospitalizations and deaths. The first trip she managed to make, after months of confinement and thanks to having vaccination certificates against Covid-19, was to Cornwall, a wonderful historic area of England, characterized by old stone buildings, cobbled streets, abundant vegetation, kilometers of hectares of greenery and mountains, added to beautiful beaches where the water is transparent when joining the English canal with the Atlantic Ocean.

During the first days of quarantine, Esmeralda, being on the verge of death, lost track of time; hours, days, and nights didn't exist for her, everything was dark, of pain and suffocation, and the obstruction of her airways had been extreme. With an enormous effort, she begged her beloved Terry to help her breathe:

–Please... please... I need air, I can't breathe... I'm suffocating... I feel like I'm dying...

Terry, with his blue eyes reddened and full of tears, with trembling hands took Esmeralda's and begged her to please not leave him, asking her to be strong, brave, as she had always been, to fight for her life, that he was there next to her, to take care of her and love her forever.

–Esmy... Esmy... my beloved Esmy, please, breathe. Look, I opened the windows wide for you, so that fresh and pure air come in from the garden. Esmy, breathe, please make an effort, our bedroom is very airy and bright…

They were days of great pain, despair and frustration for not being able to alleviate the suffering and help his beloved Esmeralda recover her health, who laid in bed, semi-sitting, with her eyes closed, without any movement. If it hadn't been for her body heat, you would have thought she was dead…

After a week, under Terry's intensive and permanent care, assisted by Esmeralda's two great medical friends, the one from Italy and the one from Chile, in addition to the NHS service with whom she communicated several times a day and every time she had a reaction, either worsening or improving, following with extreme rigor the indications for administering the medication, respecting the doses and frequencies, paying special attention to oxygen levels and fluids, Terry was forced, in the midst of the disease, to learn techniques for managing devices and medical technology, which were completely foreign to him, such as administering IV fluids and oxygen, in addition to monitoring vital signs, recording blood pressure levels and sudden rises in temperature.

The doctors insisted to Terry that the seriousness of Esmeralda's state warranted intubation, meaning her hospitalization was essential. However, he steadfastly refused to open the door to allow the NHS medical staff in when they came for her; he couldn't break the oath he had made to his beloved Esmy on her deathbed:

—My love, please... please... promise me you won't abandon me in a hospital.

—But, my beloved Esmy, the doctors are very good and they know how to cure you and restore your health.

—Noooo...Nooooo... I don't want to go to a hospital. I don't want to die in a hospital far away from you.

—Please, don't say that, Esmy, I can't... I can't see you suffer... without doing anything to help you recover.

—My love, if you take me to the hospital... you will never see me again... you know it as much as I do... I won't make it out alive from the hospital.

—Nooo... nooo... that's not true, you'll recover and we'll continue to be very happy. I'll take you wherever you want to go, no matter how far and expensive it may be, I promise.

—Nooo... that's not true, I'd like to believe that, but all those who are hospitalized die in the hospital... nooo, I don't want to die alone in a hospital, please, please.

—Nooo... nooo... Esmy, people get better and go back home to their families and you will also return, I promise.

–Noooo, you can't promise me that, not everyone is saved… I know I'm very ill and I know I'll get worse; I don't have the strength to keep fighting…

Terry threw himself on her chest and burst into tears pleading:

–Shut up… shut up… stop… stop…I don't want to… I can't keep listening to you… please… please…

–My love… we have to be strong… if I'm going to die… I want to die in your arms and not abandoned in a cold hospital room, please… please…

–Nooo… you are not going to die, we will die together, when we are old.

–Please, promise me you won't take me to the hospital, promise me.

–Don't ask me that, please, it's as if you were asking me to let you die; in that case, I rather die and not you.

–Promise me you'll always be by my side.

–I promise you, my beloved Esmy!!!

Esmeralda felt exhausted, she lay in bed drained after the great effort it took to get Terry to promise he wouldn't admit her to a hospital, and although the promise was disguised and not direct, he promised that he would always be by her side, not that he wouldn't take her to the hospital. But for Esmeralda the promise that he would always be by her side meant that physically he would always be by her side, that is, by her sickbed, at home.

Terry ran out of the room, terrified he shouted at the top of his lungs in the middle of the backyard, sobbing with his gaze fixed on the sky:

—My God... my God... why are you taking her away... why, if I love her with all the strength of my heart?!!!

When Esmeralda returned to London from Italy, and contacted Terry again without any pretext, she never imagined that death was around the corner.

After having shared almost six months with her Sweetheart, six intense months, full of pain, anguish and uncertainty, she noticed that her Sweetheart had completely melted.

Now, coming out strengthened not only from the gravity in which she was, but after overcoming an existential crisis that prompted her to throw overboard the true love of her life for a mirage, she knew and understood that love must be constantly cultivated, day by day. Passion is important, of course, and she, for a long time, mistook it for love. For years she idealized a relationship that only worked between four walls and without sharing hobbies, tastes, thoughts, goals or language, because one falls in love with the body, but also with the spirit. Their spirits were separate, without knowing it, and their bodies worked perfectly together, but they didn't have what it took to face adversity, even though she was convinced of it. They never had the opportunity to get to know each other thoroughly to express their points of view and show themselves as they were, because the language was effectively a barrier, a barrier that they thought could collapse. Love was what she thought she felt for Todd, and what she imagined she would revive in their encounter; that enormous passion of youth, which consumes, and also destroys.

That allowed her to see and feel clearly; after days and nights of deep reflection, the scale of her love had completely tipped towards Terry, and at the other end laid the melted chocolate, clearing stating:

You are no longer my Sweetheart!!!!